John & Sally McKenna's Guides

IRELAND

W9-BJK-914

WHERE TO EAT AND STAY ON THE

WILD
ATLANTIC
WAY

**written and photographed by
John & Sally McKenna**

Updated 2015

[E] Estragon Press

[E]

First published by in 2014
This updated edition published 2015
by Estragon Press Ltd
Durrus, Bantry, County Cork
Text and Photographs © Estragon Press

website: www.guides.ie

ISBN 978-1-906927-21-9

Written by John McKenna

Publishing Manager: Sally McKenna
Special correspondent: William Barry
Web: Fluidedge
Digital Editions: Dónal Mulligan
Copy Editor: Judith Casey
Editorial Assistant: Eve Clancy
Printed by Graphycems

Photographic Credits:
Leslie Williams page 90
Matthew Thompson page 91
PJ McKenna pages 81, 124 & 148
all other photos by Sally & John McKenna

Acknowledgements:
The publishers would like to thank Frank McKevitt, Edwina Murray, Chris Carroll, Paul Neilan, the Gill & MacMillan team, Hugh Stancliffe and staff at Graphycems.

For Michael Vaughan

with special thanks to our team of editors: Eamon Barrett, William Barry, Caroline Byrne, Aoife Cox, Caroline Hennessey, Joe McNamee & Leslie Williams.

Many of the places featured in this book are only open during the summer season, which means that they can be closed for any given length of time between October and March. Booking is always advisable.

We greatly appreciate receiving emails with suggestions and criticisms from readers, and would like to thank those who have written in the past, whose opinions are of enormous assistance to us when considering which people, places and products finally make the McKennas' Guides. www.guides.ie

We are on Facebook and Twitter
https://www.facebook.com/
wheretoeatandstayonthewildatlanticway
@McKennasGuides

CONTENTS

1. The Foyle Bridge, Inishowen & the Fanad Peninsula   5

2. North West Dunfanaghy to Donegal town   17

3. Sligo Bay to Erris Head & the Mullet Peninsula   25

4. Achill to Westport   39

5. Inishbofin & Connemara   53

6. Galway Bay   61

7. The Flaggy Shore, the Burren, the Cliffs of Moher   93

8. Liscannor Bay to Loop Head   103

9. Kerry Head to the Dingle Peninsula   117

10. The Ring of Kerry   131

11. The Ring of Beara   143

12. Bantry Bay to the Sheep's Head   147

13. Goleen, Mizen Head and Roaring Water Bay   157

14. Baltimore, Toe Head & Galley Head   163

15. The Old Head of Kinsale   171

Index   181

About McKennas' Guides   189

The Foyle Bridge, Inishowen & the Fanad Peninsula

In Donegal, in wintertime, the roads and trees unite in their boot-black, bible-black starkness, an ancient bog oak darkness that gives the small fields a feeling of utter, aching loneliness. Driving through the valleys, the roads feel like intrusions into a wild landscape, crawling through animate nature while the mountains maintain a snarlful eye as you run a gauntlet through them, past ferns as torchy red as the young Maureen O'Hara's hair. That lazy wind will rush straight through you and into your bones, should you decide to take a walk on the northern beaches. The light is as cold as that line from TS Eliot's *The Waste Land*: *'I will show you fear in a handful of dust.'*

Summer scatters this gloom and introversion, and one then thinks of Eliot again: *'Yet with these April sunsets, that somehow recall/My buried life, and Paris in the Spring/I feel immeasurably at peace, and find the world/To be wonderful and youthful, after all'.*
Nowhere else offers the intense brilliance of a sunset in Donegal, nothing can compete with the lurid volumes of russet and rouge light that anoint the county. The harshness and starkness of winter is repelled, the county is wonderful and youthful, after all.

Guildhall Cafés

Derry's famous 17th century landmark is a centre for social, political and cultural events. There are two brilliant cafés associated with the Guildhall – **Guild,** which is housed in the riverside entrance to the building, and **Legenderry Warehouse No 1**, which is adjacent to the main building. Guild opens onto the riverside selling snacks and drinks prepared by much-loved Bundoran restaurant The Beach House. Legenderry Warehouse is great for brunch and is proud of it's wonderful coffee. It's a funky, don't-miss! place. It also sports a very groovy shop with very smart goods to bring home from the maiden city.

Legenderry Warehouse No 1, Guildhall Street, Derry + 44 2871 264798 www. legenderrywarehouseno1. com

Guild, The Guildhall, Derry + 44 2871 360505 www.guildcafe.co.uk

⍾ Pyke 'n' Pommes

If you stroll down to Queens Quay, hard by the River Foyle, you will find Pyke 'n' Pommes, and you will have found the food truck of your dreams. You make your mind up, place your order – *The Codfather; the Notorious P.I.G; the Legenderry Burger* – you sit on a bench or you sit in your car and enjoy it, and you ask yourself: how on earth can this food, which has been finished in an old British Leyland truck parked beside a river, possibly be so good? This is restaurant quality food, this is cutting-edge food, this is magnificent food. The sourcing is superlative, and the finishing does more than justice to impeccable ingredients.

"It's a bit of theatre, having a bit of craic. That's what makes it work", says Mr Pyke, but there's more to it than that. What makes it work is Mr Pyke's passionate conviction, as well as his sourcing and his skills. *Queen's Quay, Derry +44 7594 307561 www.pykenpomes.com. Open daily.*

🚍 The Merchant House & The Saddler's House

Joan Pyne is a woman in search of an authenticity, in search of an aesthetic. Her restoration work on two major Derry properties – The Saddler's House and The Merchant's House – is valuable and important work, especially in a Province that is often fixated on the historical past, but careless about its architectural heritage. And, the breakfasts are terrific: don't miss the marmalade! *Saddler's House, 36 Gt James Street, Derry; Merchant House, 16 Queen Street, Derry + 44 2871 269691 www.thesaddlershouse.com.*

⍾ Browns & Browns in Town

Ian Orr is cooking some of the best food in Ireland right now. Browns delivers some of the most interesting, and involving contemporary cooking that you will find anywhere, yet what is instructive about Ian Orr is that his cooking is not at all didactic. His food is not grandstanding, he cooks for pleasure and comfort, not to show off, or demonstrate what a hot shot he is. It's the same in Brown's in Town, Ian Orr's second restaurant. Brown's in Town is indubitably swish, and it's a good swishness because it isn't blowsy or brash: it's subtle and restrained and, thereby, all the more enjoyable. It's the kind of room that makes you want to party, the kind of restaurant that shouts: restaurant! You might find yourself settling into one of these gorgeous booths and find, suddenly, that it is several hours later. The cooking is red hot, modern and unselfconscious, and the team deliver it with polished perfection: the staff in both Browns restaurants are uncommonly good at their work. *1 Bonds Hill + 44 2871 345180; 23 Strand Road + 44 2871 362889 www.brownsrestaurant.com. Open lunch and dinner.*

Above: Legenderry Warehouse No 1

Below: The Merchant House in the Georgian district and Pyke'n'Pommes food truck.

The Custom House
This gorgeous restaurant and wine bar looks like something straight out of central Manhattan, and its restoration has been beautifully and painstakingly achieved. Christopher Moran's menus offer an extensive tableau of dishes, all centred on properly curated foods – sourcing fish from Greencastle, 21-day aged steaks from Antrim, and chicken from Armagh, and there are lots of tasty things to tempt the appetite: crispy hen's egg with streaky bacon and homemade brown sauce; chef's lamb plate with aubergine caviar; cod with spinach and fennel potato. Stylish and very professional. *Custom House St, Queens Quay, Derry + 44 2871 373366 www.customhouserestaurant. com. Open lunch and dinner.*

Local Food
Northern Ireland is famous for its 'Home Bakeries' Be sure to ask for the local Northern Irish breads for breakfast: these include *fadge* (potato bread) and *farls* (a quick-rising soda bread, made from either white or brown flour).

Local Food

Look out for the artisan breads baked by the **Scarpello & Co** These are genuinely slow cooked in a wood-fired pizza oven. You can find them in Harry's, including the Saturday market, and The Counter and other outlets.

www.slowfood-co.com
+ 44 7793 917877 or
+ 353 74 915 6777

Harry's Saturday Market

Nothing can start your journey off along the Wild Atlantic Way better than a visit to the Saturday market at Harry's Restaurant. You'll find SlowFoodCo breads and cakes. There are splendid vegetarian pies and treats. There is the most wonderful goat meat. There is artisan pork and beef and bacon and sausages. There is the most amazing fish and shellfish from Greencastle. There are fabulous vegetables from Harry's own walled garden. In short, there is everything you need if you are preparing a picnic for the journey. And then, shopping finished, it's straight into Harry's for some delicious brunchy, zappy, tasty food and ace coffees to get the motor running. And do try this: hot Hamilton's Farm pork sausage; fresh cold Greencastle oyster, then a sip of Kinnegar ale. Ah! *Bonemaine, Bridgend, County Donegal + 353 74 936 8544 www.harrys.ie. Market open Sat morning.*

Harry's Restaurant

Donal Doherty isn't a man to stand still. Having built the weekend market at Harry's into a whizz-bang success with a thunderous array of producers, and with the arrival of the brilliant Derek Creagh, one of the most talented of Donegal cooks, as head chef, Mr Doherty lately opened Harry's Shack, in Portstewart, to riotous acclaim. The Shack takes the Harry's template of impeccable ingredients and serves them simply and perfectly. Meantime, at Bridgend, the signature style of Inishowen ingredients on an Inishowen menu produces superlative foods with superlative tastes – Greencastle queen scallops with garlic flowers and romanesco from the walled garden; mackerel ceviche with beet aioli; pork belly with pea tendrils and onion confit; trio of Dexter beef (sirloin; tenderloin; and rump) with broccoli rabe and dauphinoise potatoes; panna cotta with raspberry sorbet. The tastes and textures are vivid, bracing and beautiful, and Mr Doherty is one of the great hosts. *Bonemaine, Bridgend, County Donegal + 353 74 936 8544 www. harrys.ie. Open lunch and dinner, brunch weekends.*

Opposite: Brunch on Harry's Market day.

Below: Harry's Restaurant and Saturday market.

Doherty's Cafe

This is a lovely spot for coffee and sweet and savoury treats on the strip at Bridgend. *Bridgend, County Donegal + 353 74 938 6603 dohertyscafe@yahoo.com. Open daily.*

Kealy's Seafood Bar

Kealy's of Greencastle has always been a restaurant where seafood is treated with classical respect and restraint – haddock with a Stilton sauce; salmon with bearnaise sauce; john dory with anchovy butter; dover sole meuniere; lobster thermidor. These dishes are as unchanging, timeless and confident as is Kealy's itself, one of the country's classic seafood restaurants. Excellent local beef and lamb supplement the fish classics. *The Harbour, Greencastle, County Donegal + 353 74 938 1010 www.kealysseafoodbar.ie. Open lunch and dinner.*

McGrory's

Everyone who visits McGrory's claims a special affinity with one or other aspect of this Culdaff destination – the gigs in the Back Room; the trad sessions in the Front Bar; the friendly cooking in the bar; the enjoyment of dinner in the restaurant; the comfort of the unpretentious rooms; the charm of the staff. But for us, McGrory's is all about the siblings who power this iconic address – Anne, John and Neil McGrory. Their pure Donegal hospitality is the pivot on which everything turns, but it is also their knowledge of their county and their peninsula, and their sympathy and appreciation for the history of their business which was run by their parents and their grandparents before them, that gives a richness, complexity and truly unique culture to this brilliant place. *Culdaff, County Donegal + 353 74 937 9104 www.mcgrorys.ie. Open lunch and dinner.*

Caffe Banba

Dominic and Andrea aren't just the most Northerly baristas in Ireland, they are also the bravest. For when the wind whips around Banba's Head up there at Malin Head, at the most northerly extremity of Ireland, it blows with such force that it is a fearsome proposition to be brave enough to get out of the car. So, summon up your courage and head over for a beautiful coffee and some lovely buns and cakes from the Banba coffee bar on wheels. There is also a Caffe Banba shop in Carndonagh where you can secure that vital hit of good caffeine in more sedate surroundings. *Ballyhillion, Malin Head, County Donegal + 353 74 937 0538 www.caffebanba.com – Open daily during the summer months.*

Below: Caffe Banba at Malin Head.

Below: The Glen House

Claire The Bakers

Claire's is a little husband-and-wife-run café in the SuperValu shopping centre at Carndonagh. A great place to buy a picnic, or to stop by for coffee and a sandwich. Home-made cakes are their real speciality. *Unit 4, SuperValu, Carndonagh, County Donegal + 353 74 937 3927. Open daily Mon-Sat.*

The Glen House

Sonia McGonagle's The Glen House, in little Clonmany, way up north amidst the stunning natural beauty of the windswept Malin headland, is a beautiful house in a beautiful place. If that was all The Glen offered, that would be hunky dory. But, along with the beauty, you also get the benefit of the amazing skills of Mrs McGonagle when you stay, and this lady is one of the best hosts. Assisted by a helpful team, there are lovely rooms, and a fine tea room you can relax in after a visit to the Glenevin Waterfall. Mrs McGonagle is one of the most meticulous B&B keepers, with an obsessive attention to detail, whether it is the correct way to place sandwiches and cakes on a cake tier, or how to dress a room, or maintaining a standard of housekeeping the makes everyone happy. It is a house that pushes all the buttons, and we can't think of anything nicer than a few days here, spent walking on the beaches and on through the Urris Hills and the Mamore Gap, with the promise of the return to The Glen to end a perfect day. *Straid, Clonmany, County Donegal + 353 74 937 6745 www.glenhouse.ie.*

The Beach House Bar & Restaurant

Claire McGowan is a great restaurateur, and The Beach House is a great Buncrana restaurant. It is great because it feels right, because the food feels right, because the room seems to act almost like a tabula rasa: ready to be whatever you want it to be, whether that is a bowl of soup and a sandwich at lunchtime or a blow-out special with a bunch of friends. We can explain this effect by saying simply that Ms McGowan's focus is entirely on her customers – she is one of the new generation of hosts who are transforming the reputation of Donegal. The cooking is right on the money: a tasting plate of local crab; deep-fried St Tola's goat's cheese and beetroot ice cream; Greencastle cod with freshwater prawns; Donegal fillet steak with red wine jus; Beach House snowball. The wine list is superb, service is understated and polite, and value for money is excellent. Ms McGowan also runs Guild café at the Guildhall in Derry. *Swilly Road, Buncrana, County Donegal + 353 74 936 1050 www.thebeachhouse.ie. Open lunch and dinner.*

The Red Door

Sean Clifford has charge of the kitchens in The Red Door in Fahan, a gorgeous house with the most gorgeous location on the water's edge. It's a hugely popular wedding destination, but there are also rooms for regular guests. It's a great spot for afernoon tea, and Mr Clifford's cooking is imaginative and creative – Donegal beef with Muckish red ale and blue cheese rarebit; hake on the bone with lobster cream; pork belly with crispy pork shoulder. *Fahan, Inishowen, County Donegal + 353 74 936 0289 www.thereddoor.ie. Open lunch and dinner.*

Local Food

Philip and Sarah Moss have run Filligan's, one of the most distinctive and creative artisan food businesses in Ireland, for twenty years now. **Filligan's Preserves** are available locally in good B&Bs and shops, and they just have to be on your shopping list.
Sarah & Philip Moss, Tullyard, Glenties, County Donegal + 353 74 955 1628 www.filligans.com

Above: Richard Finney
Right: The Counter

Wild Atlantic Camp

Choose from a heated wooden camping pod, with proper beds, or stay in your own tent or motorhome. This is your base to explore Blue Flag beaches, forest parks, heritage sites, and great walking, cycling and driving routes. The beautiful location of this well-run campsite, overlooking Sheephaven Bay, means you can walk to the pub or the beach, or take advantage of the many on-site amenities.
www.wildatlanticcamp.ie

The Counter

Richard Finney has great taste. He finds all the super foods and wines that interest him, and brings them to the lucky folk of Letterkenny. There isn't a dud detail in the intriguing meshwork of foods and wines he has curated for The Counter and – best of all – Mr Finney knows how to use and amplify all the things he sells. Which means, for instance, that the Counter is where you go to for a fantastic cup of coffee to start your day, as well as that great bottle of wine. Sure, you can come in here with nothing but designs on a bottle of Pinot Grigio on your mind, but the chances are that you will leave with the Pinot Grigio, and with some Ballinasloe goat's cheese, and the benchmark standard wood-oven baked breads from Scarpello & Co., and a slice of roasted cauliflower and mascarpone tart, and a bar of Skelligs chocolate and some Gaeta olives and a cup of Badger & Dodo and a couple of bottles of Donegal craft beer, and Wall & Keogh teas and ... Phew! Got all that? The Counter has everything you need, and all those fantastic wines as well, and Mr Finney is a serious player in Donegal's food culture, a man who is making things happen way up north. *Canal Road, Letterkenny, County Donegal + 353 74 9120075 www.thecounterdeli.com. Open daily.*

Rathmullan House

After fifty years of dedicated service, Rathmullan has lately seen the biggest changes to its set-up since the Wheeler family opened their doors to the public. Michael Hurley now has charge of the kitchens in the Cook and Gardener restaurant (formerly known as the Weeping Elm), and Mark Wheeler and his team have introduced a more informal style of dining. In the basement, the radical Tap Room has been attracting droves of people for its splendiferous pizza and craft beer offering and, away from Donegal, the Rathmullan Good Food Road Van brings superb cooking to festival goers throughout the country. It's a glorious house, always romantic, and the sumptuous breakfast is one of the best you will find anywhere on the WAW. *Lough Swilly, Rathmullan, County Donegal+ 353 74 9158188 www.rathmullanhouse.com.*

The Tap Room

Kemal Scarpello of Scarpello & Co., Rick le Vert of Kinnegar Brewing and Mark Wheeler of Rathmullan House are the mighty trinity of talents whose work in The Tap Room has been drawing huge numbers of people to feast on incredible pizzas, beers and mighty craic. This is an inspired and inspiring collaboration of truly creative cooks, brewers and hosts, and should not be missed. *Lough Swilly, Rathmullan, County Donegal+ 353 74 9158188 www.rathmullanhouse.com.*

Above: Ana's famous American-style cupcakes at The Counter.

Craft Brewery

Kinnegar Craft Brewery of Rathmullan is a hard act to keep up with. One minute, Rick and his team are producing two beers. Then it was three beers. Suddenly it was five, and they fire off special brews in between times, just to stay on their toes, and to celebrate Xmas, or someone's birthday. The design of the labels and their signature cardboard carrying box is beautiful, and the beer inside is special. The five Kinnegar beers are: Limeburner, a pale ale; Rustbucket, a rye ale; Yannaroddy, their porter; Scraggy Bay, an India pale ale; and Devil's Backbone, an amber ale. They are the wine of the county, and every WAW voyager needs to try all the wines of the counties as you head along the trail, so the Kinnegar beers are the perfect place to start this exuberant exploration. Rick and the team love brewing up special occasion beers every so often, so don't miss these extra-special limited editions.
Rick Le Vert, Rathmullan, County Donegal + 353 74 915 8875 www.kinnegarbrewing.com

SCRAGGY
BAY
INDIA PALE ALE

KINNEGAR

RUSTBUCKET
RYE ALE

KINNEGAR

YANNARODDY
PORTER

KINNEGAR

DEVIL
BACKBO
AMBER ALE

North West
Dunfanaghy to
Donegal town

The Green Man

Eileen and Neil draw in lots of interesting foods from near and far in this essential shop, everything from Donegal sea vegetables to Ainé's chocolates to Glastry Farm ice cream to wines from Richard in Letterkenny's The Counter to the brilliant Filligan's Preserves. Essential. *Main Street, Dunfanaghy, County Donegal + 353 74 910 0800. Open daily.*

The Mill Restaurant

Derek Alcorn always credits his kitchen crew at the foot of his menus, a gesture that is typical of his generosity as a chef. He is a self-effacing guy, an old-school chef who stays in his kitchen and cooks great food for the happy residents of this great restaurant with rooms, and for diners. His menus are also beautifully concise and composed – half a dozen starters including a soup; five mains including a good vegetarian choice. The truth of the matter, however, is that choosing is painful: you want the lot – Irish rabbit bon bons with guinea fowl, parsnip purée, grapes and oat crumble; duck egg with goat's cheese; Cranford scallops with a pea nage and Killult spinach; Ballyare beef with banana shallot and celeriac cannelloni; Killybegs cod with prosciutto mash and a pea and buttermilk velouté; lemon tart with lemon curd macaroons and lime ice cream. Value for money is exceptional, the service from Susan Alcorn and her team is excellent, and the experience of The Mill is simply sublime. The rooms are beautiful and ageless, and the location of the house and the restaurant, beside New Lake on the edge of Dunfanaghy, is an enchantment all by itself. No wonder everyone's a regular. *Figart, Dunfanaghy, County Donegal + 353 74 913 6985 www.themill-restaurant.com*

Craft Brewery

Muckish Mountain Brewery

Janet and Leo Harkin's first beer is the nutty Miner's Red Ale, made with centennial hops and dark crystal malt. Hunt it down in good pubs throughout the county. *www.muckishmountain-brewery.com*

The Cove

This restaurant and tapas bar has an unprepossessing exterior, but there is nothing unprepossessing about Siobhan Sweeney's vivid, Asian-accented cooking. There is an Ottolenghi-like exactness about her food, and she loves the zestiness of limes and the heat of chilli. But there is also a Ballymaloe-school rootedness to her work, so it's earthy as well, and the combination makes for great eating. Peter Byrne runs the room with good humour, and there are smashing beers and wines to kick off the evening in the bar upstairs. *Port na Blagh, Dunfanaghy, County Donegal + 353 74 9136300 Open dinner.*

Starfish Café and Bistro

With its laid-back, bricolage design style, and the authentic rusticity of the cooking, Victoria Massey's Starfish Café is just the sort of destination you want to find in a seasidey place like Dunfanaghy.They cook and serve good Donegal beef, fresh local fish and shellfish, turf smoked salmon from Carrigart, and with some good music from local musicians it's very easy to linger longtime. *Main Street, Dunfanaghy, County Donegal + 353 87 32997169 www.starfishcafeandbistro.com. Open daily. Evening Bistro open weekends and in summertime.*

Olde Glen Bar and Restaurant

The Olde Glen has always been a cult destination in County Donegal for great drinks and great cooking, and continues in that exalted vein under Cormac Walsh's direction. The bar is a sure-fire classic, a true original that dates back a couple of hundred years, and which has worn those years well. Make sure to get there early in order to get a table to enjoy some excellent seafood and good, imaginative cooking in the restaurant at the back. And get Aengus to pull you a pint of Rustbucket from Kinnegar Brewery to start the evening in style. *Carrigart, County Donegal +* 083 1585777 *Restaurant open dinner.*

Danny Minnie's

The O'Donnell family's restaurant with rooms must be one of the longest established restaurants and bars in County Donegal, with a history stretching back over many generations. The dining room is grand and ceremonial, a place for special occasions, a place to enjoy Brian O'Donnell's cooking in classic combinations such as venison with celeriac purée, or Hereford sirloin with pepper, brandy and cream sauce, or medallions of monkfish with crab bisque sauce. The well-appointed rooms make for luxurious lodging. *Annagry, County Donegal + 353 74 9548201 www.dannyminnies.ie*

Nancy's Bar

How could you not love a traditional Donegal bar that describes its seafood chowder as "very fishy"! How cool is that? Well, cool is what Nancy's Bar is. It's been made famous by the hard work of the McHugh family, who have kept it the way it should be – a warren of cosy rooms – and just made it better with the passing of time, thanks to offering the best cooking they can. *Front Street, Ardara, County Donegal + 353 74 9541187.*

The West End Café

Charlie and Philomena's café is a legendary destination, known principally for their famous fish and chips, freshly cooked and a wonderful demonstration of the fryer's art. But the menu offers much more besides, and the cooking is generous and real. *Main Street, Ardara, County Donegal + 353 74 9541656. Open daily and early evening.*

Local Food

Donegal Rapeseed Oil led the way amongst the wave of modern Irish rapeseed oils, and it has pretty much conquered the country as the go-to cooking oil for both professional and domestic chefs throughout Ireland. It's health-filled DNA make it an essential part of the kitchen armoury, along with a very high smoking point which makes it splendidly versatile.

Oakfield Demesne, Raphoe, County Donegal + 353 74 914 5386 donegalrapeseedoilco.com

⫲ Tí Linn

Tí Linn is a coffee shop and craft shop which is part of the Slieve League Cliffs Centre at Carrick. You might wend your way out west to see the Bunglass Cliffs, the highest sea cliffs in Europe, but the good food, excellent coffee and beautiful crafts in Paddy and Siobhan's stylish Tí Linn will give you another reason to return, thanks to Paddy's barista skills and Siobhan's delicious cooking. *Teelin, Carrick, County Donegal + 353 74 973 9077 www.slieveleaguecliffs.ie*

🛏 Castle Murray House

Castle Murray is a restaurant with rooms, and offers some of Donegal's most jaw-dropping views out over St. John's Point. Many people order their classic dishes time after time – the prawns and monkfish in garlic butter gratinated with mozzarella, then the roast Silverhill duck breast with confit red onion purée and port jus, then the warm Belgian chocolate cake with coconut ice cream. All delicious, all good, and whilst you might point out what they are missing – the Inver Bay oysters with chive beurre blanc; the scallops with beetroot croquettes; the halibut and crab with roast butternut squash; the Caribbean trifle – part of the reason for the success of this lovely restaurant with rooms over the last twenty five years is the fact that their classic dishes are, in effect, bomb proof: they deliver them perfectly every time. Good rooms upstairs to rest your head and get ready for the next part of the WAW. *Dunkineely, County Donegal + 353 74 973 7022 www.castlemurray.com.*

⫲ The Village Tavern

Enda O'Rourke's tavern in Mountcharles is one of the guiding lights behind the Donegal Good Food Taverns. The founding philosophy and mission statement of the DGFT is not just practised in The Village Tavern, it is exemplified: Enda sources his fish and shellfish from the ports of Inver and Killybegs; he works hand in glove with Larry Masterson of the nearby Blissberry Farm to grow produce in raised beds and polytunnels, and the result is here to be enjoyed in deft and delicious cooking: summer lobster salad with marinated watermelon; pan-seared scallops with slow-braised tomato broth; seafood taster board; hand-dived scallop gratin; Drimerone lamb with pea risotto; turbot with local crabmeat. Note that you can buy the kitchen's breads and cakes to take away. *Main Street, Mountcharles, County Donegal + 353 74 973 5622 www.villagetavern.ie*

Aroma

Tom and Arturo of the invaluable Aroma, at the Donegal Craft Village, simply go from strength to strength, season afer season, year after year. For a business like Aroma, which is but a tiny single room and which is perennially packed, to show improved results every year really tells you all you need to know about one of the best places to eat in Donegal. What happens in Aroma is simple: people come here for the first time, they eat the food, buy the breads, and then they keep coming back, time and again, and the reason why is simply because it is so consistent, so good, so reliable, and the food is so delicious. Arturo cooks European staples – risotto; polenta; pasta – just as well as he cooks his native chimichangas and quesadillas – and Tom's baking is superlative: if you haven't had the Tunisian orange cake, you haven't lived. Aroma has the most dedicated customers, and everyone you meet is a regular. *The Craft Village, Donegal Town, County Donegal + 353 74 972 3222. www.donegalcraftvillage.com/aroma.html Open daily.*

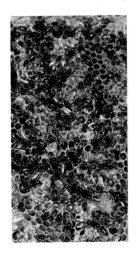

The Blueberry Tearoom

The Blueberry is a small, flower-bedecked room where Brian and Ruperta Gallagher takes care of everyone as if they were family and where tasty, clever food makes sure that everyone who visits comes back. The honesty and hard work of this couple is inspiring, and don't miss Ruperta's great puddings and desserts. *Castle Street, Donegal, County Donegal + 353 74 972 2933. Open daily and early evening.*

Craft Brewery

Don't miss Brendan O'Reilly's celebrated bar and wine shop, **Dicey Reilly's,** in Ballyshannon. It's here they run a classic bar, brew their quartet of excellent craft beers, organise the Wild Atlantic beer festival, and the wine shop is quite simply the best in the region. Not to be missed.

Market Street, Ballyshannon, County Donegal + 353 71 985 1371 www.donegalbrewingcompany.com

❯❯ The Olde Castle Bar & Restaurant

The Olde Castle is the star of Donegal town, for Seoirse and Maeve O'Toole are pushing all the right buttons here in this beautifully restored bar and restaurant. It's a place for both visitors and locals, as visitors can enjoy the good local seafoods that they hope and expect to find in Donegal – Donegal Bay mussels; lobster; Mullaghmore crab; Greencastle haddock – as well as Irish stew and Wicklow venison pie and braised Sligo lamb shank. For locals, the menus offer smart, accessible cooking – triple club sandwich; cheddar cheese beef burger; Maeve's prawn salad. And don't miss their excellent craft beer, Red Hugh Brew. *Tirconnell Street, Donegal, County Donegal + 353 74 972 1262 www.oldecastlebar.com. Open bar lunch and restaurant dinner.*

❯❯ The Harbour

Debbie and Jo offer good Donegal fish and shellfish and the rare local Aubrac beef, from butcher Eddie Walsh, on menus that are popular and accessible and in dishes which shine with their care and attention to detail. Great staff make the whole thing run like clockwork. *Quay Street, Donegal, County Donegal + 353 74 972 1702 www.theharbour.ie. Open dinner.*

🛏 The Courthouse

Unique. Interesting. Memorable. That's how people describe Piero Melis's cooking. We couldn't agree more. A recent dinner featured several dishes that were nothing other than outstanding: Mullaghmore lobster pappardella with light korma and basil sauce; incredible home-made duck ravioli with white ragu; beautiful john dory with mascarpone and crab sauce; sublime veal saltimbocca with mozzarella, Parma ham and a white wine sauce. The food was gracious, subtle and sublime. To make the most of the evening, stay upstairs in the simple rooms, and enjoy the Iselis wines from Mr Melis's Sardinia. *Main Street, Kinlough, County Leitrim +353 71 984 2391 www.thecourthouserest.com. Open dinner and Sun lunch.*

3
Sligo Bay
to Erris Head & the
Mullet Peninsula

If you are walking the beaches and headlands of Sligo and it should start to rain, don't worry. In fifteen minutes the weather will be transformed from squally showers to beaming sunshine, and instead of being soaking you will be sweating. Sligo is mercurial, always changing, always elusive, much like the mighty waves that draw surfers from all over the world to wave shrines from Mullaghmore to Enniscrone.

WILD ATLANTIC WAY

Eithna's By The Sea
Eithna O'Sullivan is the great food heroine of Sligo, and her seafood restaurant right at the harbour in Mullaghmore has served as a beacon of creative and imaginative cooking for many years. Ms O'Sullivan's seafood cookery pushes all the right buttons, often thanks to the inspired use of foraged seaweeds in dishes such as alaria baked hake, or nori sticky toffee pudding, and once you have tried the grilled mackerel with seaweed pesto, or the seaweed and blackberry compote served with some crunchy meringues, you will also want to get a jar or several of Eithna's delicious seaweed condiments to bring home. *The Harbour, Mullaghmore, County Sligo + 353 86 851 5607 www.bythesea.ie*

Seacrest Guest House
Eithna O'Sullivan also runs this comfortable guesthouse in Mullaghmore, which is only 50 metres from a Blue Flag beach. There are three rooms for guests, all fully appointed. Surfers should note that Mullaghmore is one of the top ten big wave surf spots in the world, so get the board out. *Mullaghmore, County Sligo + 353 71 9266468 www.seacrestguesthouse.com*

Lang's of Grange

Lang's is as authentic a bar as any traveller could hope to find, and the Burke family offer good pub grub – steak sandwich; fish and chips; bangers and mash – perfect for enjoying with a pint of Donegal Blonde. *Grange, County Sligo + 353 71 916 3105 www.langs.ie. Open lunch and dinner.*

Drumcliffe Tea House

The Tea House is where you go for tea and buns and some choice retail therapy when you pay your respects to W.B. Yeats in Drumcliffe graveyard. *Drumcliffe, County Sligo + 353 71 914 4956 www. drumcliffeteahouse.ie Open day time.*

Vintage Lane

All the design elements are artfully mismatched in this quirky and cute café, but the cooking and baking are straight ahead delicious, whether it's a savoury goat's cheese tart or a sweet lemon drizzle cake. There is an excellent craft and food market also held here on Saturday mornings, so that is the optimum time to pay a visit. But anytime the wind is whistling over Ben Bulben you will find a warm fire blazing in Vintage Lane and an excellent cup of coffee, served with charm and good cheer by a team who enjoy their work and who are forging a fine reputation. *Branleys Yard, Rathcormac, County Sligo + 353 87 662 2600. Open daily.*

Markets

Sligo has developed a cracking market, so look out for Irish organic meats, Bluebell Farm organic nettle pesto; J&M's veggie treats; eggs from Ballysadare; Trevor's cheeses; Organic Centre plants; Kinneden organic vegetables; Shanvaus honeys; Gerry's fish, and lots more. Just smashing.

Sligo IT Sports Field Car Park, Saturday morning.

The Beltra Country Market also runs on Saturday morning and has a coffee room as well as selling local produce, home baking and local crafts.

Harry's Bar & Gastro Pub

Five generations of the Ewing family have welcomed visitors to Rosses Point, and Fenton Ewing and his team offer good cooking, so turn up for baked Atlantic cod, venison pie, spit-roasted lamb, all made from scratch and served by a dedicated team who really enjoy their work. *Rosses Point, Sligo, County Sligo + 353 71 917 7173 www.harryrossespoint.com*

Coach Lane

Orla and Andy serve food both in the upstairs restaurant and in the bar at Donaghy's, but it's the steak frites served upstairs that brings many people back to Coach lane. Ingredients are carefully sourced, and there are good seafood choices as well as those fine rib-eyes and sirloins. *1 Lord Edward Street, Sligo, County Sligo + 353 71 916 2417 www.coachlane.ie*

Down Yonder B&B

Down Yonder is an ultra-smart B&B in Rosses Point, with fabulous views from the bedroom windows, great hospitality and a very carefully considered breakfast. There are twenty-two acres in which to roam, and the house is a gift for golfers, being just adjacent to County Sligo Golf Course - it actually overlooks the 9th hole. *Upper Rosses, Rosses Point, Sligo, County Sligo + 353 89 2103639 www.downyonder.ie*

Eala Bhan Restaurant

Anthony Gray runs both Eala Bhan restaurant in Sligo town and its sister restaurant, Tra Bhan, out in Strandhill. The cooking in Eala Bhan is ambitious and imaginative — 8-hour Sligo pork belly with chorizo jelly; pan-seared scallops with kataifi prawns and crab bon bon; duo of Sligo lamb with lamb pie and lamb rack; blackberry bakewell tart — and there is a smart, city-like room in which to enjoy their modern riffs on classic dishes. Out in Strandhill at Tra Bhan the cooking is simple and tasty. *Sligo town, County Sligo + 353 71 9145823 www.ealabhan.ie. Open lunch and dinner.*

Fabio's

Fabio's is a tiny kiosk-like shop selling home-made ice-cream, which is made fresh on site with local ingredients and fresh fruit. *2a Wine Street, Sligo, County Sligo + 353 87 177 2732 Open daily.*

The Glasshouse

The excellent central location of The Glasshouse, and the good views over The Garavogue river makes it the best choice for staying in Sligo. The staff are enthusiastic, the decor has a funky, retro vibe with lots of boldly coloured and stylised artworks and lots of lime and orange on the colour palette. *Swan Point, Sligo, County Sligo + 353 71 914 9170 www.theglasshouse.ie*

Gourmet Parlour

'We don't compromise', Catherine Farrell will tell you to explain the success of the Gourmet Parlour. 'Everything is homemade - if we make a ham sandwich the ham is boiled in house, the mayo is home-made with free-range eggs'. Aoife Cox of the *McKennas' Guides* says: 'Within seconds - seconds - I succumbed to the charms of apple tart, homemade blackcurrant jam and spinach and mushroom pie. The lure of authentic and honest baking was simply irresistible'. It has been that way ever since the GP first featured in our books way, way back in 1991. *Bridge Street, Sligo, County Sligo + 353 71 914 4617 www.gourmetparlour.com*

Opposite: Lyon's Café

Seaweed Baths

Kilcullen's Hot Water Seaweed Baths is 100 years old. A century of service, a century spent harnessing the goodness of seaweeds and sea water for the benefit of our collective health. There are other seaweed baths, but there are no seaweed baths like Kilcullen's, with its traditional steam boxes, its traditional big baths, its fresh, tangy, kelpy, sea salty seaweeds. A visit here is one of life's great pleasures.

Enniscrone, County Sligo
+ 353 9636238
www.kilcullenseaweedbaths.com

¶¶ Hargadon's

Joe Grogan and Miriam Harte and their team run a superbly managed organisation in the legendary Hargadon's Bar, one of Ireland's best-known pubs. Their reputation today is founded on cracking food and superb value. But the dishes aren't inexpensive because of low-quality ingredients: in fact, their sourcing is superb — Silverhill duck; Burren smoked salmon; Clarke's meats; Charlie Kelly's shellfish. Great wines from their own wine shop complete a happy picture. *4 O'Connell Street, Sligo, County Sligo + 353 71 915 3709 www.hargadons.com*

¶¶ Kate's Kitchen

'The impossibly well-stocked Kate's Kitchen', is how Aoife Cox describes Kate, Beth and Jane's magnificent emporium. 'All the classic artisan brands are here,' says Aoife, 'Sheridan's, Ummera, Gubbeen, Janet's Country Fayre, they were all there, along with Natasha's kale crunchies, and far cheaper than you'll get them in Dublin. It is exactly the kind of place where you would expect to find the most up-to-the-minute artisan brands'. *3 Castle Street, Sligo, County Sligo + 353 71 914 3022 www.kateskitchensligo.ie*

¶¶ Lyon's Café

Gary Stafford knows food. He understands what good cooking requires, he minds his dishes and mentors them to be as good as they can be. And the result for the devoted customers in Lyon's Café is delicious, authentic food, food with trueness and goodness, food that zings with health and energy. Lyon's Café has a bright, cheery atmosphere, the sound of happy customers enjoying today's vegetable tagine, or a steak and cheese sandwich, or a proper burger with couscous. 'Everything made for taste' we noted one day: Lyon's Café — Made For Taste. The staff, of course, are top notch. *Lyon's Department Store, Quay Street, Sligo, County Sligo + 353 71 914 2969 www.garystafford.com. Open day time.*

Osta

Brid Torrades is one of Sligo's greatest food heroes, putting delicious local foods to use every day in the most imaginative and creative way, all the way from breakfast to their super tapas menus. *Unit 2, Weir View House, Stephen Street, Sligo, County Sligo + 353 71 914 4639 www.osta.ie. Open daytime and early evening.*

Shell's Café and Little Shop

Shell's is so good that it merits a trip to Strandhill, all by itself. Jane and Myles are smart, hip and experienced, and together they bring all the best elements of their travels and their cultural accumulations to play in their café. So, head to Strandhill for Persian couscous with grilled chicken, for rainbow trout with barley risotto, for herby fishcakes with mayo and fries, for slow-cooked beef brisket with gravy. Get up early for their splendid breakfasts, and pray for sunshine so you can eat them on the deck. They have a sweet little shop, they have supper club evenings, and they have written two superb books. Shell's is everyone's favourite place. *Strandhill, County Sligo + 353 71 912 2938 www.shellscafe.com Open day time.*

The Strand Bar

The Strand is where the locals drink, it's where the surfers drink, it's where folk from Sligo come to for

a drink and a bite to eat. The owners are surfing champions themselves, but you don't need to own a board to enjoy The Strand. There is excellent music, and the place is perennially packed to the rafters, as it has been for 100 years. *Strandhill, Sligo, County Sligo + 353 71 916 8140 www. thestrandbar.ie. Open lunch and dinner.*

Strandhill Lodge & Suites

This small boutique hotel is the best choice in Strandhill, and manager David McCoy and his team look after their guests well and maintain their twenty two rooms to an excellent standard. The rooms are very comfortable and sleekly designed. *Strandhill, County Sligo + 353 71 912 2122 www.strandhilllodgeandsuites.com*

The Beach Bar

The Beach Bar is well named, for the sand from the beach actually blows right up into the car park outside the McDermott family's pub.

It's a classic, low-ceilinged, thatched cottage and was a very well-kept secret before the surfers discovered Aughris Head – when we first came here almost thirty years ago you practically had the place to yourself, save for a few locals.

That isn't the case any more, for tasty food and perfect pints and loads of surf schools bring in the crowds during the summer, and everyone wants a piece of this uniquely characterful bar. And, after the waves have hammered you, everyone is hungry for pan-fried hake with pesto and scallops with stir-fried vegetables and mussels with garlic bread. *Aughris, County Sligo + 353 71 9176465 www.thebeachbarsligo.com*

Below: The Beach Bar, Aughris

The Pilot Bar

The Pilot is a really popular pub both for drinks and for their cooking, so once you are off the surf board or out of the seaweed baths, head here for refreshment. *Main Street, Inniscrone, County Sligo + 353 96 36161 www.thepilotbar.ie. Open lunch and dinner.*

Clarke's Seafood Delicatessen

The Clarke brothers run a benchmark seafood shop here in Ballina. For decades the family has been famous for their smoked salmon, but in fact that expertise runs through every aspect of a model modern fish business, so their prepared fish dishes and their deli fish concoctions are just as fine as their wet fish and their smoked fish. *O'Rahilly Street, Ballina, County Mayo + 353 96 21022 www.clarkes.ie*

Heffernan's Fine Foods and the Heifer & Hen Café

Heffernan's seems to be a business blessed with eternal youth. It's actually more than 50 years old – established in 1961 by John Heffernan – and yet it is as hip-to-the-trip as anywhere in the West. Like so many other Mayo destinations, Heffernan's reinvented itself a few years back, adding a spiffing deli and café whilst continuing the butchery business, and upstairs now they have the Heifer & Hen Café, so head here for crab cakes with Asian slaw, baked cod with sautéed sea vegetables, silver hake with pont neuf chips and peperonata. Heffernan's is pretty much a one-stop shop for whatever you need and want. *4 Market Square, Ballina, County Mayo + 353 96 21218 www.heffernansfinefoods.com. Open lunch and dinner.*

Market Kitchen

'I can tell you very quickly and simply that I had one of the best meals of the year so far up in Market Kitchen in Ballina', writes our man out West. 'The food really was stunning, particularly considering the price. It seems to be very much a team-based effort in the kitchen, but what a team: they really have a great system going there'.

Susan and Kieran certainly have the good system going here, upstairs at Murphy Bros' famous pub, and the cooking is rockin': mushrooms à la crème; organic salmon with a leek, prawn and cheese pie; chump of lamb with polenta fried feta; Elphin pork belly with black pudding potatoes; chocolate ganache pudding with pistachio ice cream. Great value

for money, excellent food for the children, nice food downstairs in the bar, and there is terrific energy in the Market Kitchen. *Clare Street, Ballina, County Mayo + 353 96 78538 www.marketkitchen.ie. Open dinner and Sun lunch.*

Mary's Cottage Kitchen
Mary's of Ballycastle is such a sweet, old-style bakery and café, so unpretentious and welcoming, and blessed with good cooking and good baking that is agelessly enjoyable. *Main Street, Ballycastle, County Mayo + 353 96 43361*

Polke's
Polke's is a darling wee public house, with a wee shop at the front, and that wee dram on the counter in the bar at the back has your name on it. And do check out all the wonderful art works gifted by visiting artists. *Main Street, Ballycastle, County Mayo + 353 96 43016.*

Stella Maris
Frances and Terence's stellar Stella Maris country house and restaurant has been one of the catalysts of County Mayo's culinary renaissance, one of the key players in the county's invention of itself as one of the best places to visit in Ireland to find creative cooking. When we first wrote about Mr McSweeney and Ms

Kelly's country house, way back in 2003, we predicted it would be one of the stars of the following ten years. Today, Stella Maris is recognised as one of the best places to eat and stay in County Mayo and in Ireland, and it has gained that reputation thanks to the devotion and discipline of this couple. Ms Kelly's cooking, in particular, is all her own. We have described her cooking as "Proustian", for you can eat dishes here that flood your memory with delight for years afterwards. It is cooking that comforts while it delights, a country cooking that has the most complete confidence: the confidence to be simple. *Ballycastle, County Mayo + 353 96 43322 www.stellamarisireland.com*

Léim Siar

"Fantastic" was the unambiguous term Leslie Williams of the McKennas Guides used to describe his visit to Hannah Quigley's B&B, Léim Siar. What's so fantastic? Well, the setting of course, way down Erris Head at Blacksod Bay, at the extremity of the Wild Atlantic Way, the place that readers of *The Irish Times* acclaimed as the best place to go wild in Ireland. You might turn up initially for the wildness, but Hannah's fantastic cooking will be what lures you back a second time. If you know someone who makes better pancakes with maple syrup, then lucky you, because we don't, and Mrs Quigley's scones are every bit as fine. The Irish breakfast is beautifully sourced and is perfectly cooked, the fresh soft fruits from the garden will put some real wildness into your day. The house is modern and super comfortable, the perfect shelter from the storms of West Mayo. *Blacksod, Belmullet, County Mayo + 353 97 85004 www.leimsiar.com*

Talbot Hotel

The Talbot Hotel has a design style every bit as vivid as The G Hotel in Galway. Aside from the décor however, it's the ambitious and well-executed cooking in the dining room that will have you heading back to North Mayo. *Barrack Street, Belmullet, County Mayo + 353 97 20484 www.thetalbothotel.ie.*

4
Achill to Westport

The great journalist and writer John Healy was a Mayo man, born in Charlestown, and in his classic book *No One Shouted Stop* he recalls market day in the town: 'Today at the back of your mind you can still smell Wednesday... the new hay, the brown smell of the creaking egg baskets... of fresh meat... fresh herrings and dilisk, salty tanged in this inland town... the camphored black frieze of the widow woman's best coat... the smell of the horses and donkeys... of the packing from the tea chests of the travelling man with the delph and the hardware: 'everything for the home and the farm' was the chirp of the dealer who may have had a home somewhere but never saw a farm... the day and the town was a symphony of sound and smell.'

The symphony of sound and smell is back in County Mayo these days, but it is re-born, and it is vigorous and dynamic, found in cafés and shops, found in hotels and restaurants. In the last ten years, one of the best food cultures of the West Coast has been fashioned here, and it's a food culture that has really found its mojo, founded on local foods, cooked by local chefs. There is a real sense of pride about the county's food and the late John Healy – a serious food lover – would have been delighted to see the energy there is in his native county today.

WILD ATLANTIC WAY

Opposite: An Port Mor

Local Food

Cuinneog butter is a hand-made butter made from County Mayo milk, produced from a little garden unit just outside Castlebar. The Butler family have been producing this precious product for twenty five years and today it's quite widely distributed, so you often see its distinctive orange label in supermarkets. Cuinneog is also turning up on more and more restaurant menus, with the best Irish restaurants highlighting that they use this very special ingredient. They also make a very special buttermilk, which is a great treat to drink, thanks to its thirst-slaking qualities, and of course it is essential for making the most perfect loaf of Irish soda bread. The word cuinneog is Irish for churn.

Above and opposite:
Mulranny Park

🛏 Mulranny Park

The Mulranny now has chef Chamila Mananwatta in the kitchen, only the third head chef in the history of the Nephin Restaurant. Mr Mananwatta is cooking some seriously lovely food – onion and coriander pakora with curried lentil soup; Gerry Hassett's oak smoked salmon with red amaranth; Curraun Blue trout with carrot and lemongrass purée; corn-fed chicken stuffed with white pudding and chorizo with crispy poached egg. Elsewhere, the hotel is packed with walkers and cyclists marching through the Great Western Greenway, and manager Dermot Madigan and his team demonstrate at every juncture that they are masters of their art. *Mulranny, County Mayo + 353 98 36000 www.mulrannyparkhotel. ie. Open for bar lunch with restaurant opening for dinner.*

🛏 Achill Cliff House Hotel

Teresa McNamara's little hotel is a sweet, welcoming place and Ms McNamara works hard at her cooking. The menus read straight ahead, but the cooking is extremely enjoyable, especially if you have built up an appetite on the surf or hiking the cliffs. The location is brilliant if you want to golf, cycle and surf. *Keel, Achill Island, County Mayo + 353 98 43400 www.achillcliff.com*

🍴 The Beehive Craft & Coffee Shop

In summertime, it seems that all of Achill is in The Beehive, Michael and Patricia Joyce's bustling coffee shop, craft shop and restaurant. The Beehive is well-named, for this hive of activity never stops, starting with couples and groups and surfers for morning coffee, then family lunchtimes, and everyone grabs a chance to browse the shelves and find some nice crafts and clothes. Michael and Patricia have steadily and surely expanded every aspect of their essential enterprise, and it's a vital destination on Achill, and a don't-miss! on the WAW. *Keel, Achill Island, County Mayo + 353 98 43134 joycesbeehive@msm.com*

Local Food

There are a variety of unique styles of lamb to be enjoyed on the WAW, but one of the most distinctive and special is the lamb which is born, pastured and cooked on Achill Island itself. See the entry for the Calvey family of Achill, who have half a century of experience in breeding and preparing the **Mayo Blackface Mountain Lamb.**

Bervie

The sea comes close to the house at Bervie: all you have to do is walk down the garden, open the gate, and there you are on the beach. Whatever your age, it is a primal experience. The cooking chimes with the location perfectly in this B&B – smoked Achill salmon with pickled vegetables, then the magnificent Achill lamb with pea purée (no other lamb tastes like Achill lamb), and then bread and butter pudding. Bervie is as close as the Wild Atlantic Way actually gets to the wild Atlantic, and if you are a surfing dude, or a painting dude, then there is no better place than Bervie to evoke the magic of Achill. *Keel, Achill Island, County Mayo + 353 98 43114 www.bervieachill.com*

Blackfield - loveachill.com

Surf school. Café. Fashion atelier. And double-decker bus. Gerry Brannigan's Blackfield really has the lot, and this sort of left-field adventure is just what you dream of finding when you cross over to the island from the mainland with your board on the roof. Lovely coffees will bring you back to life after the waves have smashed your body and your resolve. Blackfield is a member of the great Greenway Adventures group. *Closhreid, Achill Island, County Mayo + 353 98 43590 www.loveachill.com. Open daily.*

The Gourmet Greenway

Farmhouse cheeses. Organic farm eggs. Mayo mezze plates. Curraun blue trout. Kelly's Gourmet Greenway black pudding. Murrevagh honey. Cutting-edge west coast cookery. Dana's banana butter. Marlene's chocolates. All these, and more, are the signature foods of one of the most inspired innovations in Irish artisan foods, County Mayo's **Gourmet Greenway.** Some of the producers in the GG are in, on and around the Wild Atlantic Way, and you will find their foods in shops and markets on the route. For others you would need to make a small detour – into Castlebar, for instance – to sample their delights. The Gourmet Greenway grew out of the cycling track known as the Great Western Greenway, and has since given birth to the Greenway Adventures, a bunch of outdoorsy wild guys who will teach you how to kitesurf, abseil, kayak, ride a pony, catch a sea fish, ride a mountain bike or just explore the county on foot. So, work up an appetite on a windsurf board, then sate that appetite by discovering Mayo's best foods cooked by Mayo's best cooks. It's a mighty mix of the best the county has to offer, and no visitor should miss these inspiring adventures.

Calvey's Restaurant & Wild Mint Deli

The Calvey family birth, rear and cook the unique Achill lamb, controlling every part of the operation from farm to fork. And they have been doing it on the island for over fifty years so, when you sit down in the restaurant, what you want is six-hour braised organic Achill lamb shank, served with mash. And grilled organic Achill lamb with rosemary potatoes and wild mint jelly. Yes, there are other things to eat in Maeve Calvey's restaurant, but to be able to eat organic Achill lamb from the producers on Achill Island itself is one of the great experiences of the WAW. Grainne's Wild Mint Deli is a vital stop for tasty foods to take away, and do note that you can have an prepared Achill lamb posted anywhere in Ireland. *Keel East, Achill Island, County Mayo + 353 98 43158 www. calveysofachill.com. Open lunch and dinner.*

The Chalet & Keem Bay Fish Products

Gerry Hassett has thirty years' experience as a fish smoker, focusing on organic salmon, mackerel and kippers. With his wife, Julie, Gerry also operates The Chalet which, like the Calvey family's Achill lamb business, has half-a-century of service to Achill. Unmissable destinations and unmissable tastes when visiting on the WAW. *Keel, Achill Island, County Mayo + 353 98 43157. Open dinner.*

Pure Magic at The Lodge

The Pure Magic pizzas got a big shout out when *The Irish Times* asked its readers to find the best pizzas in Ireland. But in addition to their highly-regarded pizzas there is also a restaurant and a bar and a coffee shop and some nice rooms at this activity centre. Their core activities are windsurfing and SUP (Stand-Up Paddleboarding) but they can also organise bikes, horses, you name it, all the better to build up that mega appetite for a mega-dinner, and the the sleep of the just for those who have spent the day on the waves. *Slievemore Road, Dugort, Achill, County Mayo + 353 98 43859 www.puremagic.ie*

The Kelly Kettle

Many people are surprised to hear that the legendary Kelly Kettle is actually made in Ireland, yet it has been made in Ireland by four generations of the Kelly family. 'Camping equipment for wilderness survival, emergency preparedness or disaster kits' it says on the website – and we have to add from personal experience it is absolutely essential for a family picnic day out on the beach. Once you fire it up, you will find everyone on the beach comes over to see this miraculous cauldron in action.

www.kellykettle.com

Local Speciality

Kelly's Butchers
Sean Kelly is one of the most famous food personalities in Ireland, and he has been one of the most tireless champions on behalf of County Mayo and its food culture. He inspires people in two ways – firstly, by virtue of the superb quality of his meat products and his prize-winning charcuterie creations (this is a man who can make a wedding cake out of black pudding). Secondly, he inspires by example, for he is hard-working and enthusiastic and up-for-it, improving the quality of life for everyone who gets to sample the superlative produce of Kelly's butchers. www.kellybutchers.com

The Blue Bicycle
Philly Chamber's Blue Bicycle is a beaut. The room is beautiful, the cooking and – especially – the baking is beautiful, and there is a beautiful courtyard out back for when the sun shines. The BB is just the sort of place you dream of finding on the Greenway, with delicious food that will salve your tired body, and then get you and the kids back on the saddle. But not before a slice of Princess Grace orange cake with orange and cardamom syrup and fresh cream. The sun is shining. The Greenway beckons. All is well. *Main Street, Newport, County Mayo + 353 98 41145 www. bluebicycletearooms.com Open daily.*

Kelly's Kitchen
Shauna Kelly is one of the legendary Kelly family of Newport, and she shows the same dedication to good food that has characterised her family for decades. Ms Kelly leads the front-of house team in The Kitchen, serving the iconic Kelly's pork products for breakfast, and a host of lovely things throughout the day. A pretty room, pretty cooking. *17 Main Street, Newport, County Mayo + 353 98 41647 kellyskitchennewport@gmail.com*

Newport House

Newport is one of the great Irish country houses. It is grand, serene, majestic, aristocratic, with cooking that matches all of these attributes, classic cuisine that is led by magnificent local ingredients served in a large, gracious room. Despite its grandeur, it has few airs, but many graces, and staying and eating here is a very special experience. Their tiny little bar, incidentally, is one of our favourite places in which to have an aperitif. *Newport, County Mayo + 353 98 41222 www.newporthouse.ie*

An Port Mor

In An Port Mor, chef Frankie Mallon cooks the way he is: it's his own open and generous character that comes through in the cooking. He doesn't do styles or fads or the latest thing: he cooks for himself, and of himself. What he likes to do is to arrange beautifully curated foods on a plate, almost as if he is making a mosaic. He likes sweet, unctuous tastes – pork cheeks; lobster; a crab crust on cod; sweet Mayo lamb – and this signature style makes his food friendly to eat, easy to enjoy. It isn't concerned with fashion, instead it's concerned with simple deliciousness and with offering the tastes of Mayo in one of the great rooms in Mayo. The restaurant is a series of narrow rooms presided over by genial, caring staff and with a genial, caring boss in the kitchen. The staff give off a concern that suggests that they don't simply work here: working here is part of who they are, not part of what they do. It doesn't feel like a restaurant : it feels like someone's home. And Mr Mallon doesn't cook like the standard-issue chef: he's special. *Bridge Street, Westport, County Mayo + 353 98 26730 www.anportmor.com. Open dinner.*

Below: An Port Mor

Clew Bay Hotel

Maria and Darren's family-run hotel has a family-run style, which we like. The family has a long history of offering hospitality in the town, and they offer good cooking in Madden's Bar – Clew Bay chowder; loaded potato skins; traditional fish and chips – and in the Riverside Restaurant where the cooking is more formal. *James Street, Westport, County Mayo + 353 98 28088 www.clewbayhotel.com*

The Idle Wall

Aine Maguire, who has been one of the most influential Irish cooks of the last decade, has headed homewards to Mayo to open up The Idle Wall, and her profound knowledge of and respect for traditional Irish food ways promises to be the biggest blast on the WAW. Head to the Quay to enjoy the oyster bar, the potato menu, mackerel with cally and peas, cluaisins, gull's eggs, her signature smoked haddock poached in milk with onions, salted ballach bui, a traditional summer garden salad, the Trolley of Tarts with flan and jelly and rhubarb fool and Goody, and a selection of great European wines and Irish beers. *The Quay, Westport, County Mayo + 353 98 50692 www.theidlewall.ie. Open lunch and dinner.*

Knockranny House Hotel

'Knockranny House not only serves splendid food alongside a very considered wine list but they perform the even more difficult trick of making a relatively modern five-star hotel into something akin to an old school country house hotel - and it's all down to the wonderful people working there.' That is Joe McNamee's summation of the many charms of Knockranny House, one of the key players in County Mayo's rise as a serious destination for food lovers. Yes the cooking

Above: An Port Mor

from Seamus Commons is wonderful – amongst the very best – and yes the wine list is magic. But Knockranny is really a people place, an hotel made special by the distinctive, generous and abiding welcome that the staff exude every minute of the day. That welcome pulls together all the elements of the hotel, making you feel pampered and special. If you can, then try to get here to experience some of their special themed dinners, when everything comes together to make simple magic. *Westport, County Mayo + 353 98 28600 www.khh.ie.*

Market 57
Alongside lots of good kitchen gear and pretty household goods, Market 57 has a splendid selection of local foods and other artisan treats, so it's a good place to bring your shopping list of County Mayo specialities. *57 Bridge Street, Westport, County Mayo + 353 98 27317 www.kitchencookware.ie.*

Marlene's Chocolate Haven
If Marlene's shop is a Chocolate Haven, then that must make Marlene a Chocolate Maven. So, visit the Maven in the Haven for the legendary hot chocolate, great mochas, delicious scones, and loads of chocolate treats. *Limecourt, James Street, Westport, County Mayo + 353 98 24564 www.chocolatehaven.net. Open daily.*

Kate McCormack & Sons
Kate McCormack's is a legendary butcher's shop in Westport, with a history stretching back over six generations, and a stellar reputation. It's a classic shop, white-tiled, with butcher's hooks and just the right feeling and ambience. But it's not just a butcher's, for beside the shop you will find McCormack's coffee shop, which is a lovely space in which to take nice lunches, whilst you enjoy the art in the gallery. *Bridge Street, Westport, County Mayo + 353 98 25619 www.katemccormackandsons.ie. Open daily.*

Craft Brewery

Iain and Caroline Price were the first craft brewery to be established in County Mayo for two centuries, brewing at the **West Mayo Brewery** in their home, Hill Top Farm, in Islandeady. Look out for Clew Bay Sunset, Paddy's Pilgrim Porter and Clifford's Connacht Champion. We love the fact that the brewery is based on a small, working farm.

www.westmayobrewery.com

Opposite: Cuinneog Butter

Below: Sol Rio

Matt Molloy's

Matt Molloy is a famous musician – flute player with The Chieftains, don't you know – but in Westport he is famous as a man who runs one of the nicest tradition-al pubs in Ireland. Molloy's is a classic of the genre – crowded, sociable, affable, with fabulous music every evening, and it's a great place to hunt down the craft beers of Mayo. *Bridge Street, Westport, County Mayo + 353 98 26655 www.mattmolloy.com*

Pantry and Corkscrew

Dermott and Janice have enjoyed great success in their charming, funky restaurant, The Pantry & Cork-screw, at Westport's Octagon over the last few years. Cooking for dinner service only allows them more time for prep, more time to polish the very winning style of Mr O'Rourke's cooking. He begins with terrific ingre-dients and then brings a very personal style to the food: the menu, one suspects, are the things Dermott and Janice love to cook and love to eat. Don't miss the courgette and feta fritters, their classic cheddar-and-sage burger, the Dublin Bay prawn and courgette gnocchi, and don't miss the Bocelli estate wines, as you will only find them here. *The Octagon, Westport, County Mayo + 353 98-26977. Open dinner.*

Sol Rio

Jose and Sinead are professionals to their fingertips, and they make it all seem easy in Sol Rio, their lovely restaurant and café. It's the calmness and assurance of M. Barroso's cooking that impresses so much, the way his experience shows when he allies some grape-fruit and some pomegranate seeds to a smoked duck salad, or some ricotta tortellini with local woodcock, or pheasant served with belly of pork. "Customer is king", Sinead once told us, and they put that philosophy into practice every day, and for each and every customer. Oh, and don't miss the Portguese custard tarts, the stuff of legend. *Bridge Street, Westport, County Mayo + 353 98 28944 www.solrio.ie. Open breakfast, lunch and dinner.*

🛏 Westport Plaza Hotel

Joe and Anne Corcoran's hotel is one of those destinations where things are done correctly. The greeting, the service, the cooking, the housekeeping all sync beautifully here, and the professionalism gladdens the heart. The Corcorans have a very clear vision of creating and keeping a happy workforce as the means by which you create happy guests in an hotel, and they have made this simple, sympathetic philosophy work, both in the Plaza itself and in its larger, adjacent sister hotel, the Castlecourt Hotel. There is an evident sense of commitment from the staff here and this is just the spirit you want to discover when staying in a resort hotel in a holiday town like pretty Westport. *Castlebar Street, Westport, County Mayo + 353 98 51166 www. westportplazahotel.ie.*

Opposite: Pantry and Corkscrew

Westport Markets

Westport was voted the Best Place to live in Ireland by readers of *The Irish Times* in 2013. It could also have been voted, Best Place to Have a Food Market, as the town boasts two vigorous markets each week. The country market takes place in the town hall on Thursday mornings, whilst the food and craft market lines up on the Mall beside the river, from early on Saturday morning. See you there.

Sage Westport

Shteryo Yurukov has the culinary sensibilities of a hunter and a forager. He loves the taste of saddle of rabbit. Others cook crab claws with garlic: he cooks crab claws with wild garlic. He made a foraged coastline salad for us a while back that simply blew us away with its mixture of exotica, bitterness and wildness. He makes his fettuccine with duck eggs, and will use Calvados and wild mushrooms to finish a dish of Friendly Farmer chicken. To this love of the ruddy and the feral he brings a precise technique and sensibility. The result is brilliant eating, food that is sensual and slightly crazy, yet utterly lovable. Add in Eva's charming mastery of the room, and you can see why everyone wants to be in Sage. *10 High Street, Westport, County Mayo + 353 098 56700. Open dinner.*

The Tavern

Here's a funny thing: John and PJ McKenna are having lunch in The Tavern one July afternoon, when John's phone goes. A friend is writing a piece about... The Tavern, and wants a quote! Serendipity, or what?! So, John writes back: 'I'm in The Tavern right now! Everything about it is so pristine, so uplifting, and it melds the traditional with the modern in the most seamless and aesthetic way. It's a defining example of the Irish pub repurposed and improved: all publicans and chefs should pay careful attention.' So, pay attention to the way Myles and Ruth do their thing, because these guys are experts. And here's another funny thing: John and PJ are flying back from Lisbon, and who is on the same flight? Myles O'Brien, heading home after checking out new ideas in the Portuguese capital. That's how you stay ahead. *Murrisk, Westport, County Mayo + 353 98 64060*

Inishbofin &
Connemara

The moon-struck plateaux of Connemara can play tricks on the eye of the traveller, throwing mirages into focus as you pitch, toss and turn on the roads that wind around the calm lakes, the sodden bogs and the rock-freckled fields.

Those clouds rising out of the gap between the mountains look like smoke from a forest fire: this road seems as if it is destined to pitch you right into that lake that lies ahead: those hills appear to be many miles away but then, suddenly, you are upon them, as if the intervening land had vanished beneath you.

There is no official boundary to Connemara, no final lines which call it to a halt or announce its arrival. Distances become mere speculations of the mind, and in amongst the hills there is a feeling that the separate culture of this part of the west includes its own perspective.

WILD ATLANTIC WAY

The Beach, Days Bar and B&B

Orla Day and Adrian Herlihy run this idyllic bar and B&B on Inishbofin island. They are serious about food and serious about beer, and their fantastic location and resources mean you can quite happily expect lobster on the menu, with a glass of 8 Degrees Amber Ella or a bottle of McGrath's Black to pair with it, or some Stonewell cider with supreme of chicken and Moran's of Clifden black pudding, and they do a good sweet potato gnocchi to match the sweetness of monkfish brochettes. There are cosy rooms in the B&B, nicely appointed and colourful, and Inishbofin is slowly becoming a very cult destination indeed. *The Beach, Days Bar, Inishbofin, County Galway + 353 95 45829. Open lunch and dinner.*

Local Food

The **Cleggan Seaweed Co** has always had a vision of their seaweeds as a connoisseur product, something that sits comfortably in gourmet hampers, or on the shelves of the best delicatessens. Their Sea Pickle looks like the sort of jar you would expect to buy in Fortnum & Mason. They have always demonstrated confidence and finesse with their boxes of seaweed – five varieties, which are hand-picked from the clean local shoreline and packed and sold without need of any further processing.

www.clegganseaweed.com

🛏 Delphi Lodge

Peter Mantle's country house and estate is world-renowned, a beautiful house in one of the most beautiful places in Ireland. But equally important is the fact that Delphi doesn't try to be an hotel, or to ape hotel-style service. So, instead it is quaint, a place that is comfortable with itself, which means you will be comfortable with it too. In Delphi, they know what they can do best, and their best is what they do. *Leenane, County Galway + 353 95 42222 www.delphilodge.ie.*

🛏 Letterfrack Lodge

There is a freshness and an eagerness about the team in The Lodge that is very winning. Add in nice cooking and funky rooms – and very good value for money – and you can see that this is a popular place to both eat and stay. They stick to classic dishes – Connemara lamb shank; hake with chickpeas; Killary mussels; braised beef in red wine – and the tastes are clean and lively, and it's a terrific spot if you're with a bunch of friends. *Letterfrack, County Galway + 353 95 41222 www.letterfracklodge.com*

🛏 Renvyle House Hotel

In 2013, Renvyle House Hotel celebrated 130 years as an hotel. Just consider what Ireland was like in 1883! Just consider what it was like when W.B. Yeats spent his honeymoon here, or when Black's Guide noted in 1912 that a week's residence in Renvyle cost £3, in a fine house that was "most homely and comfortable." Today, 102 years young, Renvyle remains "most homely and comfortable". It is one of the totemic west coast destinations, and certain to be on many travellers' itinerary as they navigate the Wild Atlantic Way. And Renvyle is fortunate in having two of the great practitioners of modern hospitality at its helm: manager Ronnie Counihan and chef Tim O'Sullivan. Together Mr Counihan and Mr O'Sullivan have gifted the hotel with its own special brand of excellence, a loose-limbed but apposite informality that melds perfectly with this noble house. The cooking is distinctive, and ingredients are superbly sourced. Mr O'Sullivan is a modest man, and his cooking is understated but utterly convincing. Make sure you stay at least two nights, for it's "most homely and comfortable". *Renvyle, County Galway + 353 95 43511 www.renvyle.com*

Kylemore Abbey
The restaurant and shops at Kylemore attract 350,000 visitors each year, making it the biggest tourist destination on the West Coast. *Kylemore, County Galway + 353 95 41146 www.kylemoreabbeytourism.ie.*

Above: Kylemore Abbey

Avoca
The Avoca crew are a class act, and their utter discrimination is as evident here on the West coast as in their Wicklow and Dublin heartland. *Letterfrack, County Galway + 353 95 41058 www.avoca.ie*

Rosleague Manor
Mark Foyle's house is one of the prettiest of all the Irish country houses. Pretty in pink, with the most to-die-for location and setting, it is a quintessential part of Connemara, fusing the elegant with the elemental in a sublime cocktail. *Letterfrack, County Galway + 353 95 41101 www.rosleague.com*

The Connemara Hamper
The Connemara Hamper is just that: a little space, packed chock-a-block with lovely things. Like a good hamper, it unveils itself slowly, as you come to realise just how many things Eileen and Louise have managed to pack onto the shelves. Superlative sandwiches and rolls to take away just solved your lunchtime dilemma. *Market Street, Clifden, County Galway + 353 95 21054 www.connemarahamper.com. Open daily.*

Local Pub

Paddy Coyne's Bar Tullycross
Don't miss this pub, a classic of the genre, with real music sessions. After a pint, cross the road to see the Harry Clarke stained glass windows in the Christ The King Church, Tullycross.

Opposite: The Quay House

Dolphin Beach

In Dolphin Beach, the small details are all there: the comforting pot of tea and biscuits when you arrive; perfect beds with crisp linen; beautiful books to leaf through in the front room; home-made breads and jam; the warm welcome. Clodagh Foyle has innkeeping in her blood, and it shows. She effortlessly juggles a million household tasks, and yet is always ready with a smile. Dolphin is the house in which to truly unwind. *Lower Sky Road, Clifden, County Galway + 353 95-21204 www.dolphinbeachhouse.com*

Mallmore Country House

Siobhan Hardman has taken charge of the lovely Mallmore, a charming and quietly grand historic house, dating from the late 1700's, and five of the six rooms have terrific views of the garden and the bay. Breakfast features buttermilk pancakes with smoked salmon, French toast with bacon and maple syrup, and the traditional Irish breakfast has fresh eggs from their neighbour, whilst the preserves are made with Siobhan's own home-grown apples and fruit, and it's only a mile outside Clifden. *Clifden, County Galway + 353 95 21460 www.mallmore.com*

Mitchell's Restaurant

it's not just the room that feels right in this busy Clifden destination: the service and the food in JJ Mitchell's restaurant enjoy a consistency that you don't expect in a tourist town like Clifden. A friend once described Mitchell's to us as 'the most consistent restaurant I know from visits over the last five years'. That is an incredible accolade, but the team here earn every word of it.Their people-pleasing dishes – fine fish and chips, a good chowder, crab with brown bread, good fish cakes, good lunchtime sandwiches – bring people back time and again at lunchtime, and while the evening menu is more extensive, the team show they are in full control with every plate. *Market Street, Clifden, County Galway +353 95 21867 www.mitchellsrestaurantclifden.com. Open lunch and dinner.*

Quay House

The thing about Paddy Foyle is that he does everything... wrong. When he puts a set of plates, or a set of cloches to hang on a wall, for instance, he just fires them up there and when he's finished they look... incredible. Perfect. And yet, wrong. Years ago we described him as an 'iconoclast', but in retrospect we're not sure. Iconoclasts

destroy, but Mr Foyle doesn't destroy: he just creates differently. He can see one room as a surrealist would see it, another room will be formal, yet undershot with humour and wit. Whether you reckon he's an iconoclast or a maverick, let's agree that Paddy Foyle is probably the greatest interior designer in Ireland. 'I remain in awe of the sheer exuberance and lightheartedness of these extraordinary interiors', the blogger Pamela Peterson wrote. What will also leave you in awe is the hospitality, the welcome and the cooking from Julia and her family. *Beach Rd, Clifden, County Galway + 353 95 21369 www.thequayhouse.com*

Sea Mist House

After the huge storms of winter 1998 tore the roof off her 175-year-old house, Sheila Griffin decided to remake and remodel, and to open Sea Mist as a guest Bed and Breakfast. Ms Griffin is humorous and wise, a designer with an expert eye for colour and compatibility, and the creator of particularly memorable breakfasts. With access to her own garden fruits, freshly-laid eggs and honey, she is leagues ahead of the average B&B, so what is a cliché in the hands of others feels freshly minted here, the quality of ingredients second-to-none. All told, the vitality that Sea Mist exudes is completely winning. *Clifden, County Galway + 353 95 21441 www.seamisthouse.com*

Local Food

The words 'Savage Beauty' have been bandied around to describe various locations - but the phrase was initially coined by Oscar Wilde, about Connemara. The national food of this region is **Connemara Hill Lamb**, a food which was awarded PGI status in 2007. Connemara Hill Lamb comes from a Blackfaced Horned Ewe, a rugged, adaptable animal that grazes on the particular grasses and sedges and heathers and is well suited to the sometimes punishing climate of these mountainous uplands.

Above: Connemara Smokehouse

Below and opposite: O'Dowd's Seafood Bar

Connemara Smokehouse

Bunowen Pier is at the edge of the earth, the end of the earth. To the west of Graham Robert's Connemara Smokehouse, housed in a stone building at the edge of the pier, there is the Atlantic Ocean, and nothing else. A place so nakedly elemental is just the right place for Graham Roberts to weave his magic with smoked fish. The beech wood he uses for smoking his fish in the 1946 smoking kiln he works with allows for more subtlety than oak smoking, so the Connemara Smokehouse products are blessed with a grace and subtlety, an elusiveness, the merest touch of the beech smoke. And there are no shortcuts taken here: everything is done old school, by hand, by intuition, by experience. The good news is that the smokehouse is also an economusée, so you can visit and see the artisan process as it plays out, from the filleting to the smoking to the packing. *Bunowen Pier, Ballyconneely, Clifden, County Galway +353 95 23739 www.smokehouse.ie*

Ballynahinch Castle

Patrick O'Flaherty and his team run one of the best operations in the west, and their castle is distinguished not just by great service and excellent cooking, but also by the fact that this is the most unpretentious castle on planet earth. It's a great destination, a few minutes' drive from the coast road, but be warned: arriving here, walking in the door to see the always lit fire blazing in the hearth, may delay your plans to head further south or north on the route. The telecoms mogul, Denis O'Brien, has recently bought the castle, and developments are underfoot as we write. *Recess, County Galway + 353 95 31006 www.ballynahinch-castle.com*

Angler's Return

'Not much has changed here over the year', writes Lynn Hill of the beautiful Angler's Return, one of the great Connemara hideaways. Part of that endearing old charm is the fact that Angler's Return is an 'unplugged' house: 'I still definitely keep it a TV-free zone', says Lynn, 'a house of peace and silent sounds, crackling fires and garden birdsong, but I have succumbed, reluctantly, to wi-fi for guests. I fought against it, keeping my computer hidden in the office, pretending that guests didn't need to contact their loved-ones, know the weather, check their Apps or their flights, but realised that everyone now has to be 'logged on' and 'linked-in'!!' Well, get those messages over fast, and get back to the crackling fires and the garden birdsong. *Toombeola, Roundstone, County Galway + 353 95 31091 www.anglersreturn.com.*

O'Dowd's Seafood Bar & Restaurant

Four generations of the O'Dowd family have rattled the pots and pans of this Connemara institution in beautiful Roundstone, acquiring both a national and international audience along the way. They have acquired their legendary status by serving simple, consistent, tasty food – seafood gratin; poached salmon; smoked salmon pasta; beef and Guinness stew – both in the fantastic, classic west coast bar and in the restaurant. The cooking here is just right, executed with classy confidence and a winning lack of pretention. It's splendid that they stay open all year, so even when the winter is in full flight outside, getting a seat by the fire and a pint of stout and a plate of gratinated oysters is just the thing. *Roundstone, County Galway + 353 95 35923 www.odowdsbar.com. Open lunch and dinner.*

Galway Bay

The poet Seamus Heaney described the three islands of Aran as 'stepping stones out of Europe', a precise and poetic sizing of the lonely trio's appearance on a map. There they rest, just a hop, a step and a jump away from Clare, from Galway and Connemara, alone together in the Atlantic, with New York to the west and the sallow gap that is Galway Bay opening away to the east.

Step out of Europe, onto the stones, and you are greeted with a surround of clean green sea and by limestone, limestone everywhere. Slate grey in colour, threaded here and there by green pastures, and trellised by mile after mile of dry stone walls. The writer Tim Robinson has described this eviscerated landscape: 'This bare, soluble limestone is a uniquely tender and memorious ground…. this land has provided its inhabitants – the Neolithic tomb-builders, the Celtic cashelore, the monastic architect, the fence-making grazier of all ages – with one material only, stone, which may fall, but still endures.'

If Aran is bare, Galway city is a blast of energy, a torrent of people. The City of Tribes is the only Irish city that was never conquered, and it feels that way to this day: it's a rebel place. Galway is a wild metropolis and, if that wildness gets in your blood and in your bones, you can find that you arrive here, mainline the energy, the artiness, the intimacy, and never again leave. The city doesn't just exude energy, it attracts energy, and so it's food and hospitality culture is stuffed with people who came here, promptly fell in love with the place, then opened up shop and got stuck into the business of feeding people, and making them happy.

Builin Blasta

J-me Peaker nails it, every-time. He can scramble up some eggs and top them with a turban of smoked salmon, with a little toasted bread on the side, and you will struggle to remember when you last ate something so tasty. As far as we can see, Mr Peaker always hits the taste target, with the accuracy of an assassin. He's the Jason

Above: Builin Blasta

Bourne of flavour – charming, efficient, and ruthless in getting the flavour on the plate. This reverence for tastiness – allied, it must be said, to a charming lack of pretension, and a lively, yet calm dining room with the best, on-trend sounds you can hear – explains why Mr Peaker is a local hero, and why Builin Blasta is the destination that locals will insist you must try if you are anywhere close to Spiddal. The menu in the café never changes, simply because no one will allow it to change, so every dish is, in effect, a signature dish, and every dish is cooked by Mr Peaker. So, head to the rere of the pretty craft village to enjoy a vivid offering of dishes – filo tart of goat's cheese and smoked aubergine; pork and apple salad with crispy sage; chocolate and beetroot brownie – that all share one common aim: drop-dead deliciousness. *Spiddal Craft & Design Studios, Spiddal, County Galway +353 91 558 559 www.spiddalcrafts.ie*

Local Food

Independent Brewing Kevin O'Hara makes three cracking beers in his brewery in beautiful Carraroe – a gold ale, a red ale and a pale ale, all of them vibrant, hoppy and clean tasting. Search them out when in Connemara.
http://independentbrewing.ie

🛏 Connemara Coast Hotel

The Connemara Coast gleams like a jewel, and the staff are as good as it gets – polite; charming; assured; professional. You get a sense of welcome and warmth from the second you walk in the door, and the kitchen is meticulous. Owner Richard Sinnott is one of the greatest Irish hoteliers, and his staff match him every step of the way in fashioning a truly memorable destination. *Furbo, County Galway + 353 91 592108 www.connemaracoast.ie*

🍴 Donnelly's of Barna

Donnelly's is one of the classic West Coast pubs, a characterful collation of rooms right by the side of the road at Barna, where you will enjoy some really excellent cooking. They describe themselves as a landmark, and that's not an exaggeration. So, let's order up some hake with a garlic and herb crust, the fine haddock mornay, the monkfish with bacon and leeks, and all is good. *Barna, County Galway + 353 91 592 487 www.donnellysofbarna.com*

🍴 Mulberry's

James and Deirdre Cunningham have a great room in the centre of Barna, and Mulberry's offers Mr Cunningham's original take on modern Irish food – Gilligan's sirloin with smoked tarragon butter; shellfish pan with crab claws, mussels and prawns in tarragon cream; Roscommon beef cheek with grilled prawns; organic salmon with kale and bacon; scallops with dilisk and Savoy cabbage. You can also have a simpler, tapas-style menu in the wine bar. *Barna, County Galway + 353 91 592123 www.mulberrys.ie*

🛏 The Twelve Hotel

The Twelve, a groovy, colourful hotel at the junction in Barna, west of Galway city, is a fascinating place. It's as modern as all-get-out and yet... and yet, it's actually utterly traditional, and it is utterly traditional in a uniquely Irish way. How so? It's simple. It's because the team who work with manager Fergus O'Halloran,

all work in the old Irish way, which is to say: they look after you. They are patient, funny, generous, and un-self-conscious. They make the experience of staying here utterly special and, in the bar and restaurant (and their fabulous pizzeria), you see this social genius at work at pell-mell pace, with every member of staff over-delivering, all the time. Great cocktails, too.
Barna Village, County Galway + 353 91 597000 www.thetwelvehotel.ie

O'Grady's on the Pier

Mike O'Grady's end-of-pier restaurant is atmospheric and charming, and has been consistent and reliable for many years. Seafood is their signature, and the team like to riff on the classics to show their swerve: Clare Island salmon with smoked potato purée; plaice with Killary mussels, smoked tomato and chervil butter; silver hake with smoked paprika vermouth. There are dishes apart from fish and shellfish, of course, but those are the ones we go for. The restaurant has a sister establishment, Kirwan's Lane, in Galway city.
Seapoint, Barna, County Galway + 353 91 592223 www.ogradysonthepier.com. Open dinner.

Upstairs @ West

There is a spontaneity to Martin O'Donnell's cooking that shows the work of a chef who has arrived, and it is invigorating to see him lay out his palette of foods in Upstairs @ West. Right from the pitch-perfect brown bread and all the way through seamlessly arranged tasting menus, the cook has a steady hand: ceviche of lobster with lobster bisque; carpaccio of venison with horseradish ice cream; loin of lamb with cauliflower and sweetbreads. O'Donnell uses foraged ingredients with due restraint, and you can eat 10 courses here and feel like you've snacked on a water biscuit. Wines and service match the stellar quality of the cooking at every point, and Upstairs @ West offers some of the best cooking you will find on the Wild Atlantic Way.
Barna Village, Galway, County Galway + 353 91 597012 www.thetwelvehotel.ie. Open dinner.

Opposite: The Twelve Hotel and Upstairs at West

Pizza Dozzina

Dozzina made news locally when the two-and-a-half ton Napoliforni oven was patiently manoeuvred into the lower ground floor kitchen, and Connemara traffic was brought to a standstill. Today, it looks as if Dozzina has always been there, and if there is a traffic jam in Barna nowadays it's because so many people are coming to get Dozzina pizzas, either to eat in The Twelve, or to take away. These are great pizzas, exactingly and precisely delivered. *Barna Village, Galway, County Galway + 353 91 597012 www.thetwelvehotel.ie. Open lunch and dinner and takeaway.*

Da Roberta's Ristorante & Pizzeria

The cooking in Da Roberta is effectively Italy's Greatest Hits: pizzas, calzones, pastas. It's manic, theatrical, and it's always brilliant fun. *161 Upper Salthill, Galway, County Galway 091-585808 – Open lunch and dinner. www.darobertas.com*

Gourmet Tart Company

We think the GTC in Salthill is one of the most beautifully designed eating spaces we have ever seen, reminiscent of Daylesford Organic in Notting Hill. Our editor, Eamon Barrett, writes: 'We arrived at twelve thirty for lunch and by one o'clock there wasn't a table to be had – always a sign that you're in good hands. The menu is cleverly simple: soup, sandwiches, salads and a small selection of hot food - but everything we ate was prepared with care and was tasty and satisfying. Leaving without trying some of the amazing cakes will be almost an impossibility. A superb operation that Salthill is extremely lucky to have.' *Salthill Upper, Galway, County Galway + 353 91 861667 www.gourmettartco.com. Open daily and early evening.*

Morton's of Galway

Eric Morton's store is one of the masterly pieces of culinary editing in Ireland. Mr Morton sells everything you need, and no more. He has the best of the best, and that's all he has. There is no rubbish here, no shelf fillers. Breads, vegetables, charcuterie, meat, a fantastic range of traiteur foods to take away, excellent wines. It's all here, beautifully arrayed and presented. A model enterprise. *Lower Salthill, Galway, County Galway + 353 91 522237 -www.mortonsofgalway.ie*

Norman Villa

Mark and Dee Keogh's beautiful house is one of Salthill's most famous destinations, and amongst the most stylish. They offer two rooms for B&B, as well as running an art gallery in the house. *86 Lower Salthill, Galway, County Galway + 353 91 521 131 www.normanvillagallery.com*

Oslo

Oslo is a bustling big bar and brewery, at the seaside end of Salthill. Of most interest to visitors is their superb range of craft beers, from their Galway Bay Brewery: Buried at Sea; Bay Ale; Of Foam & Fury; Stormy Port; Full Sail. The beers are superb examples of the modern brewer's art, and have hauled in award after award. The beers also match up with the modern tasty food served in the bar – bangers and mash; steak burger; salmon and haddock fish cakes; beer-battered fish. Most of the Irish craft beers are also sold, as well as a great range of international brews. *Salthill, Galway, County Galway + 353 91 448 390 www.galwaybaybrewery.com*

The Royal Villa

The Chang family's Chinese restaurants are amongst the longest-established in Galway, and their Salthill restaurant is housed in the National Aquarium. The menus are modern, accessible and pan-Asian in style, so choosing is easy. *Salthill, Galway, County Galway + 353 91 580131 www.royalvilla.ie*

 Aniar

Aniar's reputation is as outsized as its physical space is micro-sized. You might turn up here on Dominick Street and find yourself asking if this tardis of a room really has one of the finest reputations of any restaurant in Ireland. The answer is: yes. Jp McMahon and head chef Ultan Cooke create a unique cuisine, rooted in the terroir and produce of the west coast, a cuisine that unlocks the potential of every ingredient and the possibilities inherent in the wildest of combinations – monkfish with barley and langoustine sounds simple, for instance, but if you re-imagine it as the work of Albert Adria, Salvador Dali and Sonic Youth, then you get close to the sort of wild, wilful creativity that happens here. As a contrast to the incredible cooking, the room boasts low-key simplicity: everything is quiet, the staff glide around the room, there is even a baby seat for your baby. A restaurant without pretension, and one of the very best in Ireland. *53 Lower Dominick Street, Galway, County Galway + 353 91 535947 www.aniarrestaurant.ie Open dinner.*

Anton's

A stone's throw from the Corrib, Anton O'Malley's little corner room on Father Griffin Road does the good thing. Everything they make and bake is wholesome, unpretentious, true and good. We like the calmness of the crew, and you don't find places like Anton's away from Galway, so settle in with a coffee and some buttermilk pancakes, or their hot tuna focaccia, check out the art works on the wall, and mainline the culture. *12a Father Griffin Road, Galway, County Galway + 353 91 582067 www.antonscafe.com. Open daily.*

Ard Bia at Nimmos

Aoibheann McNamara and her team set benchmarks with everything they do – service; style; ambience; cooking; uniqueness; artistry. We don't use the term artistry casually: Ms McNamara and her crew are artists to their core. They just happen to produce stunningly delicious food, but what lies behind it is not just the instinct to cook, but the instinct to create something striking, memorable, distinct, inspiring. Eating at Ard Bia is like taking part in a Happening: you, the customer, becomes part of the work of art that is the daily life of this extraordinary restaurant. *Spanish Arch, Long Walk, Galway, County Galway + 353 91 561 114 www.ardbia.com. Open lunch and dinner.*

Bierhaus & Entrepans

Bierhaus is a haven for beer heads, and offers the most amazing selection of craft beers in one of Galway's great pubs. Lately, folk have also been heading here for Paul and Frank's incredible Entrepans (sandwiches), including their classic pork banh-mi, their smoked mackerel Po'Boy, the three cheese grill, the smoked bacon BLT with fried potatoes, the tofu banh-mi. The sandwiches are unlike anything else in the city, and you'd have to be in New York or Barcelona to meet their equivalents. If you think that Irish pubs = ham sandwich and Guinness, then Bierhaus & Entrepans will blow your mind. *2 Henry Street, Galway, County Galway + 353 91 587 766 Open daily.*

Galway Market

Galway's Saturday market is one of the city's greatest achievements. Mixing vital local foods with crafts and bric a brac, it winds around Saint Nicholas' church like a crazed panjandrum, a melée of colour and craic that is unmatched by any other Irish market. New arrivals have brought fresh faces and fresh foods in recent years, joining the veteran cohort who established the Saturday market as one of the most important, don't-miss! destinations in the city. You can graze happily on good foods from the cooked food stalls as you stroll around, looking at the most characterful bunch of people you have ever seen in one place at one time. And then up the stairs into Sheridan's wine bar for a glass of prosecco. Only in Galway!

Opposite: Tigh Neachtain's Bar

Above: Brasserie on the Corner
Opposite: Cava Bodega

¶ Artisan

Matt Skeffington's Artisan is an upstairs room, decorated simply and appropriately, with bentwood chairs and strings of lights. Mark Campbell's food is as smart and well thought-through as the fine collation of wines that Matt has discovered. You will also find Artisan's daily specials on offer in Neachtain's legendary bar, on the ground floor. *2 Quay Street, Galway, County Galway + 353 91 532655 www.artisangalway. com. Open lunch and dinner.*

¶ Badger and Dodo

The Fairgeen area of Galway is finally awakening from a lengthy slumber, and the first Badger & Dodo café is a bright new player in the zone. It's comfy and cool, the coffees are killer good, and it's great to see culinary creativity back in this part of Galway. *Fairgreen Road, Galway, County Galway + 353 87 0532660 www.badgeranddodo.ie*

¶ Blakes Bar

The sister bar to Brasserie on the Corner has its own menus – carrot and coriander soup; Madras-style chicken and sweet potato curry; lamb stew with barley – and it's a typically characterful and vivacious Galway pub. *25 Eglington Street, Galway, County Galway + 353 91 530053*

¶ Brasserie on the Corner

Galway's Brasserie on the Corner shows just how to do excellent, middle-market food. Chef Joe Flaherty sources from the Best-in-the-West and, in doing so, he upends all your expectations. Deli boards are beautifully composed, the food is bright with true flavours, and the cooking has an earthy tenor: good food cooked smartly and honestly and with ambition and determination. The staff are as sharp as the food and BOTC is a rare bird: a middle-market destination that is richly worth the detour. *Eglington Street, Galway, County Galway + 353 91 530333. www.brasseriegalway.com. Open lunch and dinner.*

Cava Bodega

Here's a Cava Bodega story, and it's a true one. We are standing in the lobby of the House Hotel, waiting to check out. Ahead of us is a guy whose phone rings. He says 'Hi', then he says: 'Yeah, so he recommended we meet at this place to eat, called Cava Bodega? It was incredible, absolutely incredible!'

True story, and the man on the phone was still pumped up about his Cava Bodega experience, even though it was 9.30am the following morning. But then, Cava Bodega does that. It's an intoxicating place, and the team here produce the most intoxicating Spanish-accented food. We would turn up night after night just to eat the chicken hearts, the pig's head fritters, the jamón croquettes, the salted cod cakes and the pork neck with migas and, in an ideal life, we would have the time, energy and cash to drink our way through all the wonderful Spanish wines and sherries on the list. *1 Middle Street, Galway, County Galway + 353 91 539884 www.cavarestaurant.ie. Open dinner.*

Photos: Chi

🛏 The Connaught Hotel

The Connaught is a great big, ginormous hotel, the sort of place we traditionally steer clear of. Except that this great big place is extremely well run and, if you are staying in one of their suites with your family and can use the well-equipped kitchens, then The Connaught works out at offering extremely good value for money, yet Eyre Square is only a 10-minute stroll away, and parking is free. Not an obvious choice, perhaps, but a smart one. *Dublin Road, Galway, County Galway + 353 91 381200 www.theconnacht.ie*

🍴 Chi

Andy Bandara and Catherine O'Brien operate two Chi outlets, the city centre branch in Middle Street and the take-away branch in Westside. Their dishes span the Orient, with influences and specialities from Malaysia, Singapore, Thailand, Vietnam and China, so you can run the gamut from egg fried rice to roast duck and king prawn soup hor fun with beansprouts, Asian greens and tofu. The Middle Street room is simple and homey. *2 Middle Street, Galway, & Unit 4, Westside Enterprise Park, Westside, Galway, County Galway chigalway.com + 353 91 861687 Open evenings for dinner and take-away.*

🛏 7 Cross Street

Paris has lots of little hotels where you walk through a single narrow door, then down a narrow entrance to a little reception desk and, having checked in, you climb steep stairs to the warren of little bedrooms. Olivia O'Reilly's No 7 Cross Street is one of those hotels – the narrow doorway on the street, the narrow hall, the tiny reception space, the tiny rooms, the city centre location, the bustle and noise of the city right outside your window. So, No 7 suits us perfectly, and if you like petite rooms – let's call them intimate – and cheek-by-jowl eating, then you will love this chic space on Cross Street. They also offer a rental house just across the river. *7 Cross Street, Galway, County Galway + 353 91 530100 www.7crossstreet.com*

Dela

Dela is one of the newer arrivals in Galway's restaurant quarter, opened by Joe and Margaret Bohan. They like the concept of sharing plates – an 'indoor picnic' is their lovely turn of phrase – so there are charcuterie and cheese and seafood plates, alongside smaller plates of Connemara mussels or goat's cheese salad. Evening menus have brilliantly sourced ingredients, so you can enjoy Rossaveal scallops with pork belly and Brady's Hereford steak with portobello mushrooms. *51 Lower Dominick Street, Galway + 353 91 449252 www.dela.ie. Open lunch, brunch, dinner.*

Delight

Paula Lawrence's health café is at the Kingfisher Club in Renmore, in the east of the city. Their focus is on health-giving, energising food, so there are power salads and detoxing juices, smart sandwiches and good toasted bagels. It's lovely to see a destination that balances health and satisfaction so implicitly and successfully in its food. *Renmore Avenue, Galway, County Galway + 353 91 761 466 www.delight.ie. Open daily.*

The Dough Bros

Eugene and Ronan Greaney, and their partner Laurence Enright, have gone from street food dudes to bricks-and-mortar-and-pizza-oven city dwellers in the space of a year. Once you have a taste of their pizzas, the speed of their success will be made clear: these guys get it. And along with the creativity and the precision, the Bros ladle on the humour, the music and the good drinks, and leaven it all with some straightforward weirdness: chicken tikka pizza, like? *24 Upper Abbeygate Street, Galway , County Galway + 353 87 176 1662*

Local Food

Jennie Browne has pretty well the whole of Galway slathering over her scrummy **Goodness Cakes**. 'My aim is to inspire and educate people about the value of baking. The little changes each home can make can make a difference and recreate traditions that have been passed down through generations', she writes about Bakefest, the event she organises each year, and her cakes cook up both inspiration and goodness in every mouthful. Find her at Born, Newtownsmith, Galway, just by the river. tasteatborn@gmail.com

www.goodness.ie

Dail Bar

The Dail is one of the classic Galway pubs, perenially busy with a young crowd, and it's a valuable port of call in the city as it serves good food from breakfast through to dinner. The name doesn't reference Ireland's parliament, however: it means a place where people meet to discuss and debate. *42-44 Middle Street, Galway, County Galway + 353 91 563 777 www.thedailbar.com.*

Front Door

A hugely popular Galway pub, particularly with sports fans, and with ambitious cooking – check out the Herterich's trio of pork special, for example, with braised pork belly, apple and coriander sausage and black pudding and spring onion croquette. *High Street, Galway, County Galway + 353 91 563 757 www.front-doorpub.com.*

Goya's

Emer Murray's status as the best baker in Galway has never been challenged in more than two decades. When Ms Murray opened her little store on Shop Street, she was the best. In her hip Kirwan's Lane café and shop, she remains the best, a patissier of infinite precision, exactitude and accomplishment. Nothing comes out of the kitchen at Goya's – from the simplest sandwich to the most mellifluously ethereal cake – unless it is the best it can possibly be. Goya's is endlessly inspiring. *2/3 Kirwans Lane, Galway, County Galway, + 353 91 567010 www.goyas.ie. Open day time.*

Opposite: Goodness Cakes
Below: The Dough Bros

Dunmanus
€25/kg

Smoked Gubbeen

Region:	Schull, Co. Cork
Milk:	Cow's
Rennet:	Traditional
Maturity:	4 Weeks +
Producer:	Ferguson Family

Waxed rind, firm lactic paste with mildly smoked after flavours. Giana and Tom Ferguson have been making Gubbeen since 1980. It is oak-smoked by their son Fingal in his purpose built smokehouse.

SHERIDANS
CHEESEMONGERS

€24.60 per kg

Griffin's Bakery

Saturday morning, and the queue to buy breads at Griffin's is winding down Shop Street. Jimmy Griffin's bakery is no mere food store. Instead, it is a temple of good things, and we all come here to pledge fealty to Mr Griffin's devotion to making beautiful things to eat. Mr Griffin hasn't just continued the family business. Instead, he has super-charged it, steadily broadening the list of breads and cakes, running a superb tea rooms, and yet never losing their focus on the fact that 'Bread is not bread unless it is made by an artisan bakery.' *21 Shop Street, Galway, County Galway + 353 91 563683 www.griffinsbakery.com. Open day time.*

The Heron's Rest

There is a heron. He's called Jack. In Galway, Heron's Rest means just that: the B&B where the heron – Jack – comes to rest. You couldn't make it up. Mind you, you could hardly make Sorcha Mulloy up, either. There is no more meticulous hostess in Ireland. But she's funky, too, and she creates a breakfast that has no parallel in Ireland. Last time we started with beautiful fruit salad with goji berries and yogurt, then pearl barley porridge with poached cinnamon pears and honeyed dates. We felt like we could have taken to the skies, just like Jack. *16a Longwalk, Spanish Arch, Galway, County Galway + 353 86 337 9343 www.theheronsrest.com.*

Opposite: Sheridan's Cheesemongers

Below: Tigh Neachtain's Bar

The House Hotel

The House is a super boutique hotel, with excellent rooms and staff who work hard and take their job seriously. It is popular with hen parties, mind, but we're okay with that. *Lower Merchants Road, Latin Quarter, Galway, County Galway + 353 91 538900 www.thehouse.ie*

The Huntsman

The Huntsman offers a textbook lesson in how to do middle-market food as well as it can be done. Stephen Francis and the team offer cooking that is affordable, democratic and delicious, food that appeals to young and old, food that is great on a quiet Monday and perfect on a raucous Saturday, and that is what you will enjoy in this extraordinarily successful bar and restaurant. The food on the menus reads conventional enough, for instance, but the detail in each dish is utterly different from what you would be offered in a conventional hotel, and it is the use of seeds and nuts, the use of raw salad ingredients, the confident plating and colours, the use of pickles and salads and the like to keep the mouth interested, that gives them the winning advantage. Lovely rooms upstairs to rest your head also. *164 College Road, Galway, County Galway + 353 91 562849 www.huntsmaninn.com. Open breakfast, lunch and dinner.*

Above: The Huntsman

Kai Café + Restaurant

In Kai, Jess Murphy shows that there is nothing she can't cook to its zenith of flavour and texture, no ingredient that doesn't make her mind race with a furious creativity - Silke's halloumi; goat's curd; Brady's striploin; sea buckthorn and apple sea beet hogget chops; her own labneh with dukkah; West coast crab with Green Goddess dressing. The food in Kai is not just elemental, it is instinctual, it broaches no argument in its total confidence and philosophical sureness. For many food lovers, Kai is their favourite restaurant not just in Galway, but in Ireland. David Murphy runs the room superbly, and value is excellent. *Sea Road, Galway, County Galway + 353 91 526003 www.kaicaferestaurant.com. Open lunch and dinner.*

Kappa Ya

Kappa-ya is a Celtic Japanese restaurant, and if that sounds like some kind of crazy fusion then that is exactly what it is. Junichi Yoshiyagawa interprets Celtic ingredients through the prism of his Japanese culinary skills, and the result is unlike anything you will find anywhere else. The room is tiny and when they do the magic, there is nowhere else like it. *4 Middle Street Mews, Galway, County Galway + 353 91 865930. Open daily.*

Kettle of Fish

The Kettle of Fish is the city outpost of a fine fish and chip shop that originally opened in Gort, south of the city. They make splendid fish and chips – dry, crisp, hot, flavourful, light, beautifully executed and a real demonstration of the fryer's art. Everything is cooked to order, and it's a commonplace to hear people say that Kettle of Fish make the best fish and chips. *4 Lower Cross Street, Galway, County Galway + 353 91 569881. Open lunch til late.*

The Kitchen @ Galway City Museum

A confession: when we find ourselves in The Kitchen, we can never make up our mind. Why? Because we want to eat everything. We want the aubergine and chickpea curry with curried lime yogurt. We want the citrus and coriander cured salmon with caper and horseradish potato salad. We want the hasselback sweet potatoes with buttermilk chicken. We want the chilli caramel pork shoulder banh-mi. Michelle Kavanagh and her team are infinitely cool, and they cook the coolest grub, in that uniquely cool Galway style. *Spanish Parade, Galway, County Galway + 353 91 534883 www.galwaycitymuseum.ie. Open daily.*

Above: Kai Café + Restaurant

🍴 Loam

Amongst the phalanx of brilliant creative chefs in Ireland today, Enda McEvoy is the one you would find the hardest to copy. Other chefs riff on a theme, but he deliberates and, finally, composes a fugue and variations on his culinary subjects. Everything that McEvoy, and pastry chef Conor Cockram, cook runs amok with the culinary code as they turn dishes upside down and inside out, from reindeer moss with trout roe, to beef tartare with pickled gooseberries, to raw milk junket with grilled pear. A dish of queen scallops with cauliflower and celeriac is - effectively - inverted, as the scallops become a simple bullet point of sweetness in the midst of an astonishing cauliflower purée that is draped with the thinnest sheets of celeriac you have ever seen. Tiny watercress sprigs add a shot of colour, along with trompette powder that has been dusted over. The crew are great and really up-for-it, the room suits any occasion, value for money is excellent, and Loam is inimitable: don't miss this most radical restaurant. *Geatta Na Cathrach, Fairgreen, Galway + 353 91 569727 http://loamgalway.com*

The Malt House

Is there another restaurant team that tries as hard as the crew in Mary and Paul's Malt House? These guys and girls put body and soul into their work, they give it 110% all the time, every time, and their effort makes for a thunderously pleasing destination. What is perhaps most striking is the fact that customers love the Malt House to bits: actually, the guys and girls eating here aren't customers, they are devotees, they are disciples, and we understand their faith. The cooking is delicious, the service is fantastic, and the totality of the experience of eating here is one of the highlights of Galway. *Olde Malt Mall, High Street, Galway, County Galway + 353 91 567866 www.themalthouse.ie. Open lunch and dinner.*

Massimo

Jp McMahon of Aniar and Cava Bodega does the food in Massimo, and the food is every bit as good and creative as that pedigree would lead you to expect. *William Street, Galway, County Galway + 353 91 582239 www.eatgalway.com. Food served lunch and dinner.*

Opposite: Loam
Above: The Malt House
Below: McCambridge's

McCambridge's

Other food shops have restaurants as part of the business, but no one has done it as smartly as McCambridge's. The shop itself has been an anchor for Galway's food culture for decades, but the addition of the upstairs room with Heather Flaherty's cooking drawing in the crowds has been irresistible. First things first: not having to queue on the stairs to get a table is rare. Secondly, the food is worth the wait. It's accessible, on trend and fun to eat – McGeough's smoked sausage and coleslaw on a roll with pickle; duck confit with pomegranate molasses and Puy lentils; smoked chicken salad with Cashel Blue cheese; homemade venison sausages with sauerkraut. Punchy yet refined, the food hits home sweetly, and Sunday brunch is wickedly good. See you there. *38/39 Shop Street, Galway, County Galway + 353 91 562259 www.mccambridges.com. Open day time and early evening.*

Galway Atelier

'Dramatic simplicity' is a phrase used by **Cloon Keen Atelier** to describe their products, and scents of Cloon Keen are a way of capturing everything that is lovely about this county and bringing it home to enjoy. Their fragrances, when experienced through the medium of liquid soaps or scented candles, are generous, powerful and superbly crafted.

3 Kirwans Lane, Galway
+ 353 91 565 746
www.cloonkeenatelier.com.

McDonagh's Seafood House

No one was the slightest bit surprised when *The Irish Times* loudly roared their approval of Galway's legendary McDonagh's, when the newspaper polled its readers as to which fish and chip shop was the best in Ireland. Their fish restaurant is just as beloved as the chipper, and just as busy: the room is perennially packed – just like the chip shop – and you come to McDonagh's for fresh fish, fish that they source and cook correctly, so get ready to enjoy fish dishes that they send out with confidence, consistency, and charm. *22 Quay Street, Galway, County Galway + 353 91 565001 www.mcdonaghs.net. Restaurant open dinner, Fish and Chip bar open lunch and dinner.*

Martine's Quay Street Wine Bar

Martine put a hip, smart new facade on her hip, smart wine bar in 2012, but behind the new surface, this Galway institution does what it does the way it has always done it: cooking nice food, making people happy, ensuring they come back time and time again, and doing everything with a smile. Martine and her team could coast on the tourist trade, but they don't: every day they make it new, and we salute their energy. Great wines complement the vivacious cooking *21 Quay Street, Galway, County Galway + 353 91 565662 www.winebar.ie. Open for dinner weekly, lunch and dinner weekends.*

Maxwell's Restaurant

Paul O'Meara's bistro is friendly and fun and the cooking is really spot on: tasty food with something to suit all ages and which is very affordable. *Williamsgate Street, Galway, County Galway + 353 91 568974 www.maxwellsrestaurant.ie. Open lunch and dinner.*

Oscar's Seafood Bistro

Michael O'Meara is a restless chef, a guy who is always pushing his own culinary envelope. Who else would offer wolffish with potato and wood sorrel salad. He makes a dilisk and lime leaf butter for lemon sole. He makes cassoulet with cod, and teams sea beet with sauce vierge for turbot, and allies morels with sweaty betty. His cooking is a like a chess grandmaster – always two moves ahead, always strategising his flavours. Sinead Hughes, meantime, has grandmasterly skills of her own when it comes to running the modest and welcoming room that is Oscar's: Ms Hughes is one of the very best hosts. *22 Upper Dominick Street, Galway, County Galway + 353 91 582180 www.oscarsbistro.ie. Open dinner.*

Above: Petit Delice

Petit Delice

Bread lovers will tell you that the baguette baked here in the little Petit Delice is the best in town. It is indeed very good, but then so is everything else they make and bake, and the few chairs and tables at the rere of the store make for an excellent spot for taking tea and nice sweet treats. Petit, yes, and also perfectly formed and quite delicious. *7 Mainguard Street, Galway, County Galway + 353 91 500751. Open day time.*

Providence Market Kitchen

Orla Fox and her crew run this distinctively Galwegian space with energy and verve, the freshness and chutzpah of the cooking allying nicely with the almost gallery-style vibe of the rooms. *5 St Augustine Street, Galway + 353 91 533 906*

Above and Below:
Sheridan's
Opposite: The Stop B&B

Sheridan's Cheesemongers and Winebar

Sheridan's is unique. On the ground floor is the best cheese shop in Ireland. Upstairs is the best winebar in Ireland with the best wines you can buy in Ireland and delicious cheese and charcuterie plates to accompany them. But it's not just the wines and the cheeses that make Sheridan's special: it's the atmosphere, the ambience, the staff, the electricity that happens when you put a bunch of the most interesting people in a city into one room. It's not a wine bar: it's a wine salon. *Yard Street, Galway, County Galway + 353 91 564829 (shop), + 353 91 564832 (wine bar) www. sheridanscheesemongers.com.*

37 West

'Healthy is the new sexy' is Gill Carroll's guiding slogan in the funky 37 West, and judging by the success the café has enjoyed in its first year, Galwegians agree. Gill uses the excellent Les Petits Douceurs artisan breads, makes smashing breakfasts – don't miss the breakfast burrito – and whilst there is a healthy focus to everything, that doesn't mean there aren't big, satisfying flavours here, it just means it's smart cooking. *37 Lower Newcastle, Galway, County Galway + 353 91 524122 www.37west.com. Open daily.*

Tigh Neachtain

Galway has lots of good pubs, but it's hard to beat Neachtain's for that sepia-tinted, low-lit, always-4pm-in-the-afternoon feeling. One of the great classic pubs. *17 Cross Street, Galway, County Galway + 353 91 568820 www.tighneachtain.com.*

The Stop

The Stop has the most singular aesthetic, explained by the fact that Russ Hart and Emer Fitzpatrick were both gallerists in a previous life, so every detail of the house is showcased at its best, from the pictures on the wall, to the buffet table, to the food on the breakfast plate. Bathe it all in the bright light of a Galway morning and you have a superlative destination. What you don't see is the hard work that Russ and Emer have poured into the place, since they opened in 2005. It's only been in the last year, however, that The Stop has been finally completed to their liking, as they have tweaked and polished and perfected. What they aim for, they have said is a "very calm, beautiful energy", and they deliver that in spades. This is one of those breakfast rooms where everyone in the room is SO HAPPY to be here, right now. Everyone is practically gurgling with delight. It's poignant, and the energy is infectious. *38 Father Griffin Road, Galway, County Galway + 353 91 586736 www.thestopbandb.com.*

Tulsi

A tiny room with a big menu that delivers excellent Indian cooking is the Tulsi signature. It's modest and simple, the service is wonderful, the cooking always consistent and enlivening. *3 Buttermilk Walk, Middle Street, Galway, County Galway + 353 91 564831 www.tulsigalway.com. Open lunch and dinner.*

The Salt House

There are 150 bottled artisan beers for sale in this beautiful bar, and some 23 craft beers and ales and stouts on tap, so you step in the door and basically step into Beer Heaven. The crew are purist – there are no beers whatsoever from the corporate brewers – but they aren't didactic about it, so if you are bewildered by the amazing choice, simply ask what they recommend and hitch a ride to Beer Heaven. And be careful with their Of Foam and Fury Double IPA: it's a monster! *Ravens Terrace, Galway, County Galway + 353 91 441550. Open pub hours.*

Local Speciality

Les Petites Douceurs are up early in the morning to make specialist, artisan baguettes and Viennoiseries, and you can find them in good restaurants and markets in the County.

Il Vicolo

Gerry McMahon and his Il Vicolo team have relocated to a beautiful space in the Bridge Mills building, a trio of stone-clad rooms where the River Corrib rushes right underneath you. Their signature style of northern Italian small plates – chicchetti – and larger plates is rock-steady and invigorating, with lots

of citrus notes brightening dishes like classic liver and onions; burrata with grilled peaches; bacalao on grilled polenta; stuffed courgette flowers. The wines are fabulous, the service is smart and hip. *O'Brien's Bridge, Galway, County Galway + 353 91 530515 www.ilvicolo.ie. Open lunch and dinner.*

Vina Mara

Eileen Feeney has overseen Vina Mara for more than a dozen years now, and has exhibited superlative professionalism all that time. The cooking is wonderfully moreish – warm seafood pot with crusty bread; chicken with arancini; pork cutlet with Dungarvan ale – and Vina Mara also offers great value. *19 Middle Street, Galway, County Galway + 353 91 561610 www. vinamara.comOpen lunch and dinner.*

Opposite: Wa Café
Above: Il Vicilo

Wa Café

Everything you love about Japanese food – the use of colour; the sense of proportion; the deep wisdom; the quiet focus on nutrition; the enlivening hit of umami flavours – can be found in the small, intimate space that is Yoshimi Hayakawa's Wa Café. Ms Hayakawa and her crew prepare beautiful food – simple, soulful, wabi-sabi – and serve it with grace and passion, bringing Tokyo to the Corrib. *13 New Dock Street, Galway, County Galway + 353 91 895850 www.wacafe.net. Open daily to early evening.*

Kinvara Market

Music plays, chickens (such handsome chickens!) cluck, people ramble from stall to stall in the walled garden, shopping and eating and chatting and admiring the chickens, and there is everything from Sri Lankan curries to seaweed to local honey to handsome sweaters. Kinvara is a lovely, left-field market: do not miss it!

Behind Johnston's Hall, Main Street, Kinvara, Friday 10am

¶ Basilico

Paolo Sabatini knows both the Italian art of cooking, and the Italian art of eating. He knows that to cook well, you must first source your foods with precise care, so his menus celebrate the West Coast champions. And with these peerless foods at his fingertips, he then weaves that culinary magic that ushers in the 'gift of making art out of life', as Marcella and Victor Hazan describe this marvellous alchemy. Mr Sabatini's skills are best shown in dishes like 'culurglones' alla Cagliaritana, where he fills ravioli with potato, onion and Pecorino cheese and tops it with a rabbit ragu. As a statement of cucina povera it is hard to beat – simple, earthy and gutsy ingredients ennobled by gracious, patient cooking. But then he will blindside you with a simple panciotti with lemon and herbs that is so ethereal that you seem to have passed from Calabria and gone straight through to Rome. *Main Street, Oranmore, County Galway + 353 91 483693 www.basilicorestaurant.ie. Open breakfast, lunch and dinner.*

🛏 Coach House Hotel

The Basilico team do the cooking for the Coach House Hotel, and it's rock-steady. *Oranmore, County Galway + 091 353 91 788 367 www.coachhousehotel.ie*

¶ Kate's Place

At the top of the escalator in the Orantown Centre you will find Kate Wright's sweet little café. Her room is bright and girly, with a small counter of delicious things begging you to come and taste them – bakewells; apple pies; Tunisian orange cake – and lots of tables and chairs out front on the concourse. In the evening, Kate conducts various cookery classes. *1st floor, Orantown Centre, Oranmore, County Galway + 353 86 6066494 www.galwaycookeryclassses.com*

¶ Claire's Tearooms

It would be great to have Claire Walsh's singular, special tearooms and shop as your local, rather than experiencing it as a roadside stop in Clarinbridge when heading south or north on the WAW. Ms Walsh's Tearooms is a little oasis of civility and culture, with vibrant cooking, and a singular aesthetic that makes you feel better as soon as you step in the door. *Clarinbridge, County Galway + 353 91 776606. Open daily.*

Rustic Grub

'Real food to me is truly knowing where your food comes from and preserving the integrity of that food in the simplest, tastiest way possible.' You can't argue with this wonderfully commonsensical thesis of Maria McNeela, the chef-proprietor of Rustic Grub, especially when she puts that thesis on a plate and puts it in front of you: unctuous country tastes of honey-roasted duck, and game terrine, and salt and pepper sprats with lemon mayonnaise, and Galway goat's cheese pizza, and kale and scallion mash. Lovely. *Sherry's Bar, Clarinbridge, County Galway + 353 08 363 7357 www.facebook.com/rusticgrub. Open Fri-Sun.*

Moran's Oyster Cottage

Yes, Moran's is an international tourism staple, with photographs of this pretty water's edge cottage a fixture of every guide book, but it's famous because it's good, reliable and professional, and because they know what they do well and they do it as well as they can. Catherine Moran is the seventh generation of the family to run this beautiful bar. *The Weir, Kilcolgan, County Galway + 353 91 796 113 www.moransoystercottage.com. Open lunch and dinner.*

The Tide Full Inn

Marianne and her husband, Joseph, serve good honest Italian food in this lovely old pub in the centre of town. They keep things nice and tight, with a short list of starters, a few pasta dishes and a few main courses. Their signature pizzas are not just good, they are echt and delicious. And don't miss the fine baking – Rocky Road; orange and polenta cake. A super place. *Main Street, Kinvara, County Galway + 353 91 637400 www.thetidefullinn.com. Open lunch and dinner.*

Above: Moran's Oyster Cottage
Opposite: Basilico

Opposite and below:
Ruairi and Marie-Thérèse
de Blacam, Inis Meáin
Restaurant and Suites

Local Food

Look out for
**Cáis Gabhair
Árann** a new Goat's
Cheese from the Aran
Islands made by Gabriel
and Orla. They make a
soft cheese flavoured
with Dillisk seaweed,
and a Gouda-style hard
cheese from their herd
of Nubian and Saanen
goats.

Inis Meáin Restaurant and Suites

Ruairi de Blacam's cooking in the other-worldly Inis Meain restaurant echoes the manifesto of Christian Puglisi, of Copenhagen's Relae restaurant: 'We want the dining experience at Relae to be simple and unpretentious, focusing solely on gastronomy.' Mr de Blacam is aiming for the same concentrated focus on the magnificence of his island ingredients, so each plate of the 4-course dinner, served to just 16 diners each evening, has just two elements – lamb and peas; crab and rocket; lobster and wild garlic; potatoes and onions. de Blacam calls this unadorned style, 'Elemental eating', whilst Puglisi calls his 'stripped to the bone.' We call it 'Mindful cooking and eating', and there is nowhere in the world better to enjoy the pure and elemental joy of food than in this unique, unforgettable, island destination. *Inis Meain, Aran Islands + 353 86 826 6026 www.inismeain.com*

An Dún

Potatoes from the garden. Fresh mackerel. Carrageen pudding for dessert, another lovely day as you enjoy dinner in Teresa Faherty's simple B&B and restaurant. Mrs Faherty has been looking after guests here since 1989, and doing so with grace and sympathy. *Inis Meain, Aran Islands + 353 99 73047 www.inismeainaccommodation.com*

Kilmurvey House

To understand Aran requires one thing: time. So, book into Treasa and Bertie's lovely house. Swim in Kilmurvey Bay. Trek the island. Explore Dun Aengus. Enjoy Treasa's breakfasts. Enjoy Bertie's hospitality. Get a bike, and ignore the van drivers at all costs. *Kilmurvey, Inis Mór, Aran Islands + 353 99 61218 www.kilmurveyhouse.com.*

7
The Flaggy Shore, the Burren, the Cliffs of Moher

The seizing and shifting of the ages has given us not just the appearance of the Burren in County Clare, but also the secret of the Burren. It looks naked, but is profuse with life. It looks invincible but, in fact, it is being eroded and eaten all the time, every second. 'Boireann may be a rocky place, but water, not rock, is the essence of The Burren' writes E. Charles Nelson in his book on the wildflowers of the area. 'Water brought the rock into existence; aeons later frozen and running waters fashioned the karst landscape. Water moreover, will be The Burren's ultimate destroyer.'

WILD ATLANTIC WAY

Here is another sign of the hidden Burren, for underneath the stone is an underworld of caves. The play between limestone and water which produces the karst means that the water of the Burren runs underground. There are many turloughs, places where the water, mysteriously, will be one day present and the next day disappeared.

Take a tour through the honeycombed tunnels of the Aillwee caves and one sees the decisive, tireless destruction carved out by the subterranean water, in the powerful falls of the streams as they pummel the soft stone, how all of this magnificent natural intricacy will, one day, be worn to oblivion. Underneath the karst, that grey, schismed pavement with its secret wealth of flora, the stone is being steadily, ceaselessly disemboweled.

And this is the ultimate secret of the Burren. It exists as it is because it is balanced, at the end of the land and the edge of the sea, made of rock that was once eroded from above and is now being eroded from below. It is barren in appearance, but uniquely fertile.

Opposite: Burren Smokehouse

Café Linnalla

Roger and Brid Fahy make gorgeous artisan ice creams using the milk of their own herd on their own farm, and a visit to their café to enjoy the ices – and lots of other nice things – is one of the great treats of the WAW. You need to walk 2kms across the beach to get to the café, and it's worth every step to build up that appetite. *New Quay, County Clare + 353 65707 8167 www.linnallaicecream.ie*

Above: Wild Honey Inn

Granny's Coffee House/Hazel Mountain Chocolates

Kasha and John Connolly have created one of the hottest destinations in the Burren, a brilliant meld of coffee house, chocolate factory and tasting rooms that amounts to one of the essential places to visit in North Clare. Mrs Connolly is a trained chocolatier and a third-generation baker, and what chocolate-lovers need to know is that their Hazel Mountain Chocolate is bean-to-bar, the rarest artisan food you can find in Ireland. But it's not just superlative sweet things – there are also wisely-sourced savouries and soups to enjoy before you bite into that dark chocolate truffle cake with lemon curd cream, and then it's time for the chocolate shop and some 88% single estate Venezuelan. *Oughtmara, Belharbour, County Clare + 353 87 9903000 www.hazelmountainchocolates.com*

The Burren Perfumery

We have to confess that on our latest visit to Sadie Chowen's Burren Perfumery, we actually took pictures of their new outdoor loo. Why? Because like every other detail of this inspiring place, it is a little piece of classic design. But then, everything here is classic: the perfumes, of course, but also the gardens, and especially the cooking, which is pure and true – they make a potato and leek soup here that would sustain the nation, and the baking is first class, as are the splendid staff. *www.burrenperfumery.com*

The Russell Gallery

We are big fans of the lovely wines Stefania Russell imports from her native Italy, served along with coffees and organic teas and scones and smoked salmon and antipasto plates, in the aesthetic comfort of Stefania and Andy's delightful gallery, in gorgeous New Quay. Mrs Russell selects her featured artists well, and Mr Russell's raku pottery is sublime. *New Quay, County Clare + 353 65 7078185 www.russellgallery.net*

Aillwee Cave

Everything about Aillwee Cave is superbly managed. The design, the structure of the tours, the charm of the staff, the good food in the café, the hawk walk and birds of prey area and, of course, their rather special shop. You shop here for their own Burren Gold cheese, but over the years their range has increased exponentially, so now you come for the cheeses, and the fudge, and the ice cream and much more. *Ballyvaughan, County Clare + 353 65 707 7036 www.aillweecave.ie*

L'Arco

The Quinn family offer some really good, ambitious and authentic Italian cooking in the classically-styled L'Arco, and the restaurant has been the vital culinary destination in Ballyvaughan since they opened. *Main Street, Ballyvaughan, County Clare + 353 65 7083900 www.burrenrestaurant.com*

An Fear Gorta

'I don't think I've ever seen anything like it!' said Eamon Barrett when he walked into Jane O'Donoghue's tea rooms and spied the display of delights set out on the big table in this lovely room. Cakes with fruit, chocolate, coffee, cheese, caramel, toffee – you name it. If the baking is fantastic, the service matches it, making for one of the great Ballyvaughan destinations. That's Stephen Spielberg over there, isn't it? *Pier Road, Ballyvaughan, County Clare + 353 65 7077023 www.tearoomsballyvaughan.com*

Wild Sea Veg

'Hand harvested, hand packed', says Gerard Talty, explaining the stunning quality of **Wild Irish Sea Veg.** Mr Talty might have also pointed out that four generations of the family have harvested vegetables from the sea, so experience and knowing discrimination play their part. These are outstanding products, benchmark examples of each variety, all beautifully packaged, and there is no easier nor better way to get vital, mineral-rich sea vegetables into your diet.

www.wildirishseaveg.com

Opposite: Gerard Talty, Wild Irish Sea Veg

🍴 Burren Fine Food & Wine

Don't miss Cathleen's roadside operation as you climb or descend the twisty Corkscrew Hill. Not only is the cooking really fine, but service is gracious and sincere. So, a pizza for you, some lemon drizzle cake for me and are we happy? More than. Quite lovely. *Corkscrew Hill Road, Ballyvaughan, County Clare + 353 65 7077046 www.burrenwine.ie. Open day time.*

🛏 Gregan's Castle

'I wasn't expecting this to be the meal of the year', said the man at the adjoining table to ours, in the dining room of Gregan's Castle. 'But it's definitely the meal of the year', he said again. Many others will agree with him after they have finished eating David Hurley's cooking at Gregan's. There are elements of his cooking that are new, drop-dead classics – the lobster lasagne that comes with pan-glazed halibut; the puffed salmon skin with cured Clare Island salmon; the roasted onion jelly with pea velouté; the potted shrimp raviolo with butter-glazed cod; the gingerbread crisp with foie gras and duck terrine; a dark chocolate gateau so fine that our notes read 'Off the chart!!!'. It's all off the chart, to be honest: this chef is in the moment, and he is cooking in one of the most singular destinations in Ireland. Over the last several years, Simon and Freddy Haden have made Gregan's into one of the most admired destinations in Europe, a tone poem of perfection that every WAW traveller has to try. *Ballyvaughan, County Clare + 353 65 7077005 www.gregans.ie*

🍴 O'Lochlainn's Bar

O'Lochlainn's is one of the most beautiful bars in Ireland. Intimate, zen-like, handsome, and with a jaw-dropping selection of whiskeys, it is probably the Irish pub we would most like to be locked into. Time stands still from the second you walk through the narrow green doors. Unique. *Ballyvaughan, County Clare + 353 65 7077006 www.irishwhiskeybar.com*

Ballinsheen House

Terrific housekeeping and hearty breakfasts mean that the handsome Ballinsheen House, just on the edge of Lisdoon', is a perfect stop for anyone pausing on the WAW to spend a few days hiking and exploring the area in depth, or maybe discovering more about JRR Tolkien's Burren history. *Lisdoonvarna, County Clare + 353 65 7074806 www.ballinsheen.com*

The Burren Smokehouse

Brigitta Curtin's Burren Smokehouse is one of the great European smokehouses, with some of the best smoked fish you can possibly eat, so do make this little detour off the WAW into Lisdoonvarna and treat yourself. *Kincora Road, Lisdoonvarna, County Clare + 353 65 7074432 www.burrensmokehouse.ie*

Above: The Roadside Tavern

Sheedy's Hotel

The Sheedy family's hotel is a modest delight, a place where everything is made from scratch, and where the hospitality matches the excellence of the cooking. When you stay here you understand what a true 'family-run' hotel is. *Lisdoonvarna, County Clare + 353 65 7074026 www.sheedys.com*

Wild Honey Inn

Aidan and Kate's Wild Honey Inn has enjoyed spectacular success over the last five years, as befits a wonderful destination with inspired cooking and excellent, inexpensive rooms. The Wild Honey may seem like little more than a simple, classic bar, but the cooking will knock your socks off: this is some of the best food in the West, and not just at dinnertime but at breakfast time also. *Kincora Road, Lisdoonvarna + 353 65 7074300 www.wildhoneyinn.com*

Classic Pub

The **Roadside Tavern**

Peter Curtin's pub is a west coast classic, and the arrival of his own craft beers, which Peter created and began brewing in 2011, has made a great pub even greater. Lovely music sessions, too, and nice, proper cooking with good ingredients all add up to one of the best bars in the West. *Kincora Road, Lisdoonvarna www.roadsidetavern.ie*

Cullinan's Restaurant & Guest House

James and Carol Cullinan's restaurant with rooms in the centre of Doolin offers good cooking – sea bream with smoked salmon and spring onion risotto; marinated Burren lamb with a spring roll filled with confit shank of lamb, and good breakfasts will set you up for that promising day ahead. *Doolin, County Clare + 353 65 7074183 www.cullinansdoolin.com*

Hotel Doolin

Hotel Doolin is distinct, dynamic and different. There is a true sense of creativity about how the team here carry out their work, and it means that they are avoiding the clichés that make so many hotels humdrum, avoiding the by-the-rulebook mantra that makes staff in hotels so dissatisfied. And all the while they are hosting craft beer festivals, writing festivals, music festivals. Stay here and you catch that energy, and it's pretty irresistible. The cooking uses many elements from their garden, and is very fine. *Ballyvoe, Doolin, County Clare + 353 65 7074111 www.hoteldoolin.ie*

Roadford House

Frank and Marian show exactly how to run a restaurant with rooms, here in the ever-reliable Roadford House. A genuine welcome, some simple, smart accommodation, and some wowee! cooking from Mr

Sheedy that shows his mastery of west coast ingredients. Put them together, and you have an archetype of the coaching inn, the welcome retreat for the WAW traveller. The cooking is direct, elemental, and precise: this food hits the target, especially the desserts. *Doolin, County Clare + 353 65 7075050 www.roadfordrestaurant. com. Open dinner.*

Sea View House

A pretty house, overlooking the river and overlooking the pretty village of Doolin. Niall and Darra grow their own fruits for breakfast, collect eggs from their own hens, and count the food miles on each of their breakfast main dishes – the Full Irish has 50 food miles, the goat's cheese frittata has 20, the orange cinnamon French toast has

1100, but hey! – and you have a smashing place to rest your head. *Fisherstreet Doolin, County Clare + 353 87 2679617 www.seaview-doolin.ie*

Vasco

You look at the blackboard menu in Vasco and say to yourself: this is wise food: locally caught plaice with lemon and olive oil; Lebanese-style Burren lamb flatbread with cumin and mint; slow-cooked organic goat with rosemary and bean hotpot (a critic's dish if ever we saw one); very berry Bakewell with ice cream. The food refuels you, it banishes the fatigue of the road. As you happily work your way through that chicken, Gubbeen, chorizo and roasted red pepper pie you find that you are thanking your lucky stars, for you have found the Aleph, the point from which the WAW makes complete sense, the point at which your hopes and wishes are not just satisfied, but are exceeded in every way. Ross and Karen do the magic in Vasco, they are a singular pair, with a singular way of working with the foods of the west coast. *Fanore, County Clare + 353 65 7076020 www.vasco.ie. Open lunch and dinner.*

Opposite: Doolin Hotel

The Cliffs View Café

Sometimes there are so many visitors at the beautiful Cliffs of Moher that it can almost seem as if it's compulsory to have it on your itinerary. It isn't compulsory, but it is advisable, for the cliffs are truly stunning, and the café has tasty cooking and amazing views. www.cliffsofmoher.ie

8
Liscannor Bay
to Loop Head

The myth that locals will tell you when you are on the Loop Head is that there is a hidden city – Cill Stuifín – which was submerged in an earthquake some time ago, round about the fifth century.

Only Loop Head could claim to have a hidden, submerged city as part of the Wild Atlantic Way. They'd never think of that down in Dingle, or in West Cork.

Hidden, it may be. Submerged, it may be. But, in the style in which you come to expect things in south County Clare, it seems that Cill Stuifín can be glimpsed, every seven years.

Except, you don't want to gaze at it, because doing so will bring you bad luck.

Only Loop Head could claim to offer you the most spectacular, incredible vision known to man, but then tell you not to bother looking at it.

This sort of phantasmagorical craic, this audaciousness, is one of the reasons so many of us love Loop Head. It's different. It's mythic, and they make their own myths.

WILD
ATLANTIC
WAY

Bay Fish and Chips

Just as you come into Liscannor from the north, you will find the much-admired Bay chipper, and it's a great stop to refuel with tasty, zappy food for the family. *Main Street, Liscannor, County Clare + 353 83 1123351*

Egans

You could lock us into Egan's anytime you like, and leave us alone to explore the fantastic, oh-so-classy clarets and other great global wines which the Egan family have collected, and which adorn the shelves of this most beautiful bar. If your tastes incline more towards the grain than the grape, it's a great place for a quiet drink, or a noisy session. A unique destination. *Liscannor, County Clare + 353 65 7081430*

Vaughan's Anchor Inn

If you wanted to summarise Denis Vaughan's cooking in a single dish, you could scarcely do better than 'Sean Digger's lobster, sautéed foie gras, apple, pistachio, tomato.' This is the kind of thing you get at Vaughan's, rich imaginative food that comes as a surprise when you first walk into the bar and the dining room. You might have been expecting fish and chips and mushy peas, and suddenly you are offered 'Cod in a 9-year-old starter batter, chips steamed then fried in beef dripping (hooray for beef dripping!), homemade tartare sauce, pea purée.' This sense of surprise, the juxtaposition of a traditional Irish pub with this resolutely modernist food, is part of the joy of Vaughan's. *Main Street, Liscannor, County Clare + 353 65 7081548 www.vaughans.ie. Open lunch and dinner.*

Vaughan Lodge

Michael Vaughan is a dynamo, with energy levels that makes him seem ever youthful. A decade on from the day when they opened the doors of Vaughan Lodge, and Mr Vaughan has a volubility that would put a 20-year-old to shame. He is in thrall to the business, the business of running a great hotel, the business of serving great food. His secret is that Mr Vaughan is always looking ahead. There is a story we like, about a meeting with some of the west coast guys to talk about future tourism developments. At the meeting Michael Vaughan talked about and later wrote about the idea of marketing the West Coast as an entity, as a coherent, inclusive destination, and he reckoned it might be called The Atlantic Way. Just another one of his good ideas. Vaughan Lodge is one of the defining destinations on the WAW. *Ennistymon Road, Lahinch, County Clare + 353 65 7081111 www.vaughanlodge.ie*

Moy House

There are a small number of houses that inspire in the guest the earnest desire to do sweet nothing. Moy House is one of those places. You want to sit at the dinner table and enjoy the stunning cooking of Matt Strefford, whose dish of St Tola goat's cheese tortellini with pine nuts, raisins and brown butter was one of our standout dishes of 2014. Mr Strefford is a major talent, and will soon be a well-known one. Yes, yes, there is a world going on outside the walls of Moy House but, frankly my dear, you don't give a damn about that world. You are in the world of Moy House, and it is sufficient for the day. *Lahinch, County Clare + 353 65 708 2800 www.moyhouse.com*

O'Looneys on the Prom

O'Looneys is a handsome modern room with great sea views, and the cooking – Thai green curry; ham panini with a bowl of tomato and pepper soup; deep-fried hake and chips, were what we enjoyed on our last visit – is accessible and enjoyable. *The Prom, Lahinch, County Clare + 353 65 708 1414 www.olooneys. ie. Open lunch and dinner.*

Real Bread

Considine's Bread
Every town in Ireland used to have a bakery like Considine's of Kilrush. But the others have vanished whilst Considine's has thrived. The guys bake in the back of the shop and sell their breads from the shop, as well as having a van on the road to deliver to local businesses in south Clare. They have survived because they bake simply wonderful breads.

Above: Images of Ché, who stayed in The Strand Hotel, Kilkee when travelling the Wild Atlantic Way.

🍴 Morrisseys

Hugh McNally has transformed this lovely pub in Doonbeg from a traditional Irish bar into a svelte restaurant with rooms, yet he has managed to keep the ambience of the old place, where four generations of the Morrissey family have plied their trade. The cooking is modern and informal – chicken Caesar salad; Angus beef burger; salmon and cod fish cake; home-made scampi with tartare sauce – food that you can relax with, and there are also excellent rooms upstairs if you want to make a night of it. *Doonbeg, County Clare + 353 65 905 5304 www.morrisseys-doonbeg.com. Open lunch and dinner.*

🍴 Diamond Rocks

The views from the Diamond Rocks Café out over Kilkee Bay are simply stunning. Whilst it's a lovely stop-off as you walk the coastal path, it's also a fine destination in its own right. And do check out the Richard Harris statue! *West End, Kilkee, County Clare + 353 86 3721063 www.diamondrockscafe.com. Open day time.*

🍴 Lir

Deirdre Daly is mistress of all the skills. She is a superb baker, and a great patissier. She cooks like an angel, whether she is fashioning one of her celebrated gourmet sandwiches, or slowly bringing together a drop-dead delicious mushroom risotto for a Saturday night dinner. She has the confidence gifted by precise and effective technique, so she seems to have time to do everything just so, to finish every dish just the way it needs to be brought to perfection. When you add in the fact that the views from the terrace and the dining room at the golf course are amongst the best in Europe, then you know that Lir Restaurant really is one of those unforgettable gems that you stumble upon in a charmed life. Ms Daly is a power in the land, and she is going to be very famous indeed. *11 O'Connell Street, Kilkee, County Clare + 353 65 905 6075. Open daily.*

🍴 Murphy Blacks

Cillian and Mary are two of the most important players in the Loop Head food community, and Mary's cooking showcases the great fish and pristine ingredients of the region with stunning success – Loop Head seafood zarzuela; Atlantic cod with curried leeks and saffron cream; her legendary casserole of mushrooms; a classic lobster bisque; gratinated sole stuffed with crab meat – whilst Cillian looks after everyone with great charm, and great stories. Murphy Black's is a most charming restaurant, and one of the real stars of Kilkee. *The Square, Kilkee, County Clare + 353 65 905 6854. Open dinner.*

🍴 Naughton's Bar

Elaine and Robert offer some fine, expert cooking in the beautiful series of rooms that is Naughton's, with a leaning towards fish and shellfish, abetted by a selection of cracking meat dishes. They focus on getting excellent ingredients and showing them proper culinary respect, and the result is so successful that it's often impossible to get a table here, either in the bars downstairs or in the beautiful dining rooms upstairs. Naughton's is one of the great West Coast bars, but get here early, or make a booking for upstairs, or you will be sorely disappointed. *45 O'Curry Street, Kilkee, County Clare + 353 65 905 6597 www.naughtonsbar. com. Open dinner.*

Opposite: Stella Maris
Above: Murphy Blacks

The Pantry Shop & Bakery

Imelda's café and bakery can seem to be the very epi-centre of Kilkee on a busy summer day, with everyone calling in to eat breakfast, buy breads and cakes, sit around over a lazy lunch or read the paper over a cup of coffee. We suspect many Kilkee holidaymak-ers are in and out of The Pantry several times a day, starting with a berry dazzler and a wee Irish in the morning, then coronation chicken salad for lunch, and a cup of tea and a slice of carrot cake as eve-ning draws in. *O'Curry Street, Kilkee , County Clare + 353 65 905 6576 www.thepantrykilkee.com*

Stella Maris

Stella Maris is a treasurable old resort hotel, and Anne Haugh and her family do a brilliant job of looking after their guests. The rooms are cosy, the cooking is very, very good, and the sense that this is an hotel for the community is precious. It's also a completely unpre-tentious place, where everyone does their job as well as they can. We once stayed here for several days in January, and even in that quiet, off-season lull we had a terrific time. *O'Connell Street, Kilkee, County Clare + 353 65 9056455 www.stellamarishotel.com*

The Strand

Johnny and Caroline Redmond's cooking and hos-pitality in The Strand is true, spirited, and blessed with that lovely County Clare generosity. The dining room looks out on the bay – for us it's San Sebastian in microcosm – whilst the views from the bedrooms upstairs are amazing. Johnny's cooking is tasty and direct – Jack Kelly's sirloin; hake boulangere; lingui-ni with Atlantic prawns; a mighty burger with superb onion rings. The new coffee bar is a great addition to The Strand, whether you seek an Americano or a craft beer. Che Guevara stayed here back in 1961, don't you know. True, and he signed himself "Rafael Trujillo" in the visitor's book. *Kilkee, County Clare + 353 65 9056177 www.thestrandkilkee.com. Restaurant open dinner.*

Local Food

Kilbaha Gallery
Liz Greehy and Ailish Connolly are two mighty women, and they are blessed with good taste, so everything they have curated from County Clare to fill their gallery at Kilbaha is only beauti-ful and highly covetable. The gallery is also where you stop off for that vital cup of coffee when touring the extremity of the peninsula.
Kilbaha
+ 353 65 905 8843

Above: Carrigaholt Fishing and Glencarrig B&B

Post Office

Carrigaholt
When in rural areas like Loop Head on the WAW, check out the local post office, who sometimes sell local breads and cakes and veg. Carrigaholt PO is especially good for foods and crafts.

🚪 Thalassotherapy Centre Guest House

Eileen Mulcahy harvests the serrated wrack seaweeds she uses for her seaweed baths with her own hands, and then uses them to brew up the most sublime bath you have ever had. Book one of the five comfortable rooms upstairs, enjoy a delicious breakfast in the dining room, then plunge into that old porcelain bath tub for an hour, and you never felt so good in all your life. Wicked fun. *Grattan Street, Kilkee, County Clare +353 65 905 6742 www.kilkeethalasso.com*

🚪 Old School House B&B

Ian and Theresa have brought a near-derelict old national school building back to life, and offer cosy beds, and Ian's fine baking for breakfast, just on the eastern edge of Cross village. The breakfast room is a light-filled former classroom, just the right space to enjoy some fresh pancakes or maybe some freshly-caught mackerel. Ian and Theresa between them know everything that is happening in Loop Head – Teresa is actually a guide at the Loop Head lighthouse – and this is a charming spot run by charming people. *Cross, Carrigaholt, County Clare + 353 86 1549402*

Glencarrig B&B

Mary Aston is one of the best bakers we have encountered in years. Mrs Aston bakes in the Irish vernacular style, that sweetly-savoury style that blesses scones and cakes and pastries with a maternal style – simple, yet precise, designed to please. Of course, it's a very comfortable house, and Mrs Aston is a great hostess, and the house is set in a beautiful part of beautiful Loop Head, and Mr Aston takes you fishing in his boat so, yes, there will be fresh mackerel for breakfast – Glencarrig is actually the accommodation side of Carrigaholt Sea Angling Centre. But all the while you are doing all these things, you keep thinking about the lightness of the scones, the sweetness of the cakes, the pleasure that a great baker gives to the world. Mary Aston is a treasure, and we're betting she is going to be a culinary star. *Ramona, Carrigaholt, County Clare + 353 65 9058209 www.fishandstay.com*

The Long Dock

Think of the highest standards you can discover in Irish food, then take a drive way down the Loop Head to Carrigaholt, park on the big wide street and marvel as Tony Lynch shows how he can match those standards, dish by dish. The brown bread is superlative; the chowder is a classic; the fried fish is stunning; the fish pie is sheer class. The fact that you are enjoying this cooking in a great pub that is traditional yet utterly of-the-moment, with good music, a roaring fire, and great service, means the Long Dock is truly a standard setter in south west Clare. Imelda Lynch marshals the room with ease, and the Long Dock is a classic.*Carrigaholt, County Clare +353 65 9058106 www.thelongdock.com. Open lunch and dinner.*

Purecamping

Purecamping is an eco-campsite which offers both pre-erected bell tents, or a wild camping experience for those who want a more remote experience. Yoga classes available on site. *Querrin, County Clare + 353 65 9057953 www.purecamping.ie*

Below: The Long Dock

Lighthouse

Loop Head Lighthouse
The lighthouse at the tip of Loop Head offers spectacular holiday accommodation, and can be rented from the Irish Landmark Trust. Loop Head, County Clare + 353 1 6704733 www.irishlandmark.com.

🍴 Cafe Noir

Pat O'Sullivan has fashioned a great success in his Cafe Noir destinations, three handsome, comfortable rooms with particularly well-chosen food, from their excellent rustic breads - white; baguette; cheese and onion, and lots of pretty pastries - to daily staples like James McGeough's magnificent lamb and pork sausage rolls, steak and Guinness pie, good eggy quiches and nice bespoke salads. The formula is smart, the discipline is considerable, and service from cool staff is right on the money. The Cafe Noirs don't miss a beat. *Robert Street, Limerick, County Limerick + 353 61 411222 www.cafenoir.ie*

🍴 Cornstore

"It was a delight to eat there, and the staff were brilliant." We get messages like that about Cornstore all the time, and this Limerick champion simply goes from strength to strength, with a great team who really enjoy their work. *19 Thomas Street, Limerick, County Limerick + 353 61 609000 www.cornstorerestaurantslimerick.ie*

🛏 No 1 Pery Square

Patricia Roberts has been busy over the winter in No 1 Pery Square, rejigging the style of their first floor restaurant, which is now named Sash. The style of food has altered – 'home cooking with an extra layer

Opposite: Mortell's

of sophistication', says Ms Roberts — and the menus are wonderfully moreish and well-conceived: mussels with ham hock and Longueville House cider; braised cheek of Hereford beef with bourguignonne sauce; O'Loughlin's rib-eye with shallot tarte tatin; pear tarte tatin. The wine list is a masterwork — concise, original in its organisation; with a splendid selection of bottles — and the hotel itself is cosseting and comforting, and simply the best place to stay in Limerick city. *Quarter, Limerick, County Limerick +353 61 402402 www.one-perysquare.com*

Freddy's Bistro
Liz Phelan and Caroline Kerley run a great show in Freddy's, and have done so for many years. Like the best great sister 'n' sister teams, they seem effortlessly professional, utterly in control. They source and cook lovely food, and they don't mess about with it, so flavours are true and clean and the dishes are classic combinations: mushroom risotto with Parmesan; chicken with herb stuffing and red wine sauce; crab linguini with white wine sauce; sticky toffee pudding with vanilla ice cream. *Theatre Lane, Lwr Glentworth Street, Limerick, County Limerick + 353 61 418749 www.freddysbistro.com*

Gasta Good'n'Healthy
With an emphasis on healthy, gluten-free, paleo and vegan dishes, Jeff Treacy's Gasta is a great addition to Limerick. There is good funky stuff like Fit Fish Fingers, served with sweet potato chips and kale and pea mash, or Moroccan meat balls made with turkey meat and served with power salad. Healthy, and delicious. *6 Thomas Street, Limerick, County Limerick + 353 61 419171 www.gastafood.ie*

Mortell's
Brian Mortell's city centre seafood restaurant and deli doesn't have customers: it has champions. The Mortell's Champions will tell you, quite simply, that you won't find better seafood anywhere else. And,

like faithful apostles, they take their mantra from Mr Mortell himself, so if he says today's fish is black sole and he proposes the way in which he would like to cook it, then they simply assent, let Mr Mortell get on with the cooking, and wait in delighted expectation. The great thing is that the expectation is always satisfied: Mr Mortell cooks with devilish accuracy and astuteness, whether he is preparing a full Irish breakfast for you, or cooking today's catch with some sautéed potatoes and vegetables and maybe a little salad. *49 Roches Street, Limerick, County Limerick + 353 61 415457 www.mortellcatering.com*

Canteen

Hardened restaurateurs fall hard for Canteen. They see the simplicity that envelopes Paul William's little tabernacle of a restaurant, and they say: "Genius!" Mr Williams brings to Canteen exactly what it needs, and no more. He is a supremely intelligent restaurateur, a man who has brought home all the lessons he learnt at restaurants like The Fat Duck, and then simplified them, and improved them. If Heston could see what Paul is doing now, in Canteen, he would be filled with envy. The focus is on the food, and the food is ace: sublime fish taco; the felafel wrap with parsley hummus; chickpea stew with honey and pomegranate; gobi chicken curry with brown rice; green eggs and ham for brunch. Brilliant drinks, brilliant vibe, and a ground-breaking destination. *30 Mallow Street, Limerick, County Limerick + 085 7342320 www.weare-canteen.com*

La Cucina

Lorraine and Bruno have created the most iconic destination in Limerick, and just one taste of their superlative Italian cooking will show you why people drive from miles around to get these pastas, pizzas and sweet things. From a little shoebox of a room, La Cucina has expanded mightily, but the attention to detail, the precision and the craft, never slips. The staff are also the most delightful bunch of people. *5 University Court, Castletroy, Limerick, County Limerick + 353 61 333980 www.realitalianfoodies.com*

Aroi

The food in Aroi is as bright as the decor of this corner room on O'Connell Street, so head here for snappy Malaysian cooking: satay chicken on skewers, fish baked in banana leaves – the signature dish, and always a good choice – squid with squid ink sauce, red duck curry. Eddie Ong Chok Fong and his team are confident and charming and the easy-going format makes Aroi a good stopover. *1 O'Connell Street, Limerick, County Limerick + 353 61 311411 www.aroi.eu*

The Wild Onion

Rob and Ruth Di Giralamo have been supplying the city of Limerick with wonderful baking for a lost-count number of decades. Their American-style cookies, cakes and loaves are as funky and characterful as the Di Giralamos themselves. Limerick would be a considerably poorer place without this loveable destination. *Ennis Road, Limerick, County Limerick + 353 61 325555 www.wildonioncafe.com*

Milk Market

The Limerick Milk Market

The Milk Market is where you head to for some of the best eating in Limerick – superb coffees, brilliant baking, seriously fine savouries, and a plethora of the best marketeers and market stalls. So, get some Silver Darling fish, Adare Farm pig on a spit roll, a Piog pie or two, Killowen apple juice, a Country Choice cheese selection, and lots, lots more. Just make sure you have plenty of time to see everything, including the many stalls that sell arts and crafts and clothes.
www.milkmarketlimerick.ie

Opposite: La Cucina (above) The Wild Onion (below)

Kerry Head to the Dingle Peninsula

In Kerry, beauty is all before you, but it is fleeting, a magical illusion that pulses and vanishes, then re-appears, rearranged. Around the Ring the light will spangle magically on the sea, then change to coat the waves with grey and subdue them, so suddenly they seem as smooth as velvet. After the rains come the illusory rainbows, sometimes so harshly coloured that they appear to be flames of light shooting from the land.

The kaleidoscope of colours and sensations changes every instant, and one can gaze simultaneously at a valley smothered by rain and cloud and, to east or west, find a bay dappled in pools of sunlight and bright with colour. The effect is entrancing, but also enliven-ing. Kerry air seems super-charged, invigorating, filled with energy. Up the Reeks or around the ring, you find this crazy energy, which the local dialect, a blur of singing vowels, echoes.

WILD ATLANTIC WAY

Below: Rigney's Farm meats

Restaurant 1826 Adare

Wade Murphy is doing something very interesting in 1826, in Ireland's loveliest village, Adare. He is cooking delicious food, of course, and he is blessed with good judgement, so there is never more on the plate than is needed, and the courses glide from punchy starters to satisfyingly narcotic sugar confections for dessert. So far, so good, but it's the gentle, casual style of the room and its winning informality that seems to us as much the signature of 1826 as the food itself. This has to be one of the most relaxing places to eat in Ireland, and in effecting this Mr Murphy has done something which is quietly revolutionary. He has worked in grand places, so now he shuns grandeur for intimacy: he doesn't want any nonsense getting in the way of you, the customer, having a great time eating great food. 1826 is a real sweetspot. *Main Street, Adare, County Limerick + 353 61 396004 www.1826adare.ie Open dinner.*

Wild Geese

If Adare is the prettiest village, then The Wild Geese is surely the prettiest restaurant. David Foley's cooking is intricate, but beautifully realised, and service from Julie is as good as it gets. *Rose Cottage, Adare, County Limerick + 353 61 396451 www.thewild-geese.com. Open dinner and Sun lunch.*

Daroka

Dan O'Brien is a mighty chef, with a sure and profound wisdom when it comes to cooking. With his wife, Emily, working out front, his food in Daroka is simple and true: hake with pancetta and leeks; his signature chicken with sweet corn; duck with beetroot and orange. Set to be a star destination. (Cliff Road, Ballybunion, County Kerry + 353 68 27911 www.daroka.ie)

Above: Restaurant 1826 Adare

John R's

Just off the Tarbert ferry and need a good cup of coffee and something nice to eat? Then the detour into the pretty, literary town of Listowel will take you to John R's, where Pierce Walsh and his team will look after you with aplomb: nice food, nice people, and some excellent wines to take away with you. Do note that Mr Walsh also offers some excellent self-catering accommodation in a townhouse close to the café and shop. *70 Church Street, Listowel, County Kerry + 353 68 21249 www.johnrs.com*

Above & below: Rigney's Farm

McMunn's of Ballybunion

Greg and Una McMunn have been doing the good thing in their eponymous bar and restaurant with rooms in little Ballybunion for more than a decade now. The cooking is straight-ahead tasty – oysters from the tank; seared scallops with Athea black pudding; Hereford beef sirloin; lobster thermidor. *Main Street, Ballybunion, County Kerry + 353 68 28845 www.mcmunns.com*

Sundaes Ice Cream Parlour

Ballybunion is golfer territory, but for food lovers it's where you come to get a bumper ice cream, and maybe a doughnut and a cup of coffee, from Joanna McCarthy's excellent ice cream shop. *Main Street, Ballybunion, County Kerry + 353 86 0523089. Open daily.*

Darcy's

Helena has the great fortune to have the meats from
her own butcher's shop to use in the pretty Darcy's
restaurant, and she supplements these great meats
with fish from the best County Kerry suppliers. Darcy's
is particularly notable for its excellent lobster menu, a
real rarity. *Barracks Lane, Tralee, County Kerry + 353
71 94625 www.darcysbistro.com. Open dinner*

Kingdom Food & Wine

Pat and Maeve's shop is a treasure trove of good
speciality foods and some excellent foods-to-go, so
turn up at Oakpark for good coffees and freshly made
sandwiches. *Oakpark, Tralee, County Kerry + 353 66
7118562 www.kingdomstore.ie. Open daily.*

Manna

Claire and Thomas run the most splendid organic
store here on Strand Street, so if you have a picnic
planned for somewhere along the WAW, then you
need to head in to Manna for smashing organic foods
from local producers. A great store packed with truly
great foods. *Island of Geese, Strand Street, Tralee,
County Kerry + 353 66 7125699 www.mannaorgan-
icstore.ie. Open daily.*

Mary-Anne's Tea Rooms

What could be nicer than tea in Mary-Anne's, with a
warm fire blazing in the hearth and china cups and
tiers of cupcakes and hot chocolate for the young
ones. *17 Denny Street, Tralee, County Kerry + 353 87
6241837 Open daily.*

Quinlan's Seafoods

The Quinlan family have their own fleet of boats to catch their fish, so the fish they offer is as fresh as it can possibly be, and it makes their Kerry shops and restaurants, especially the smart Tralee room, really great choices. And after you have selected what fillet you would like to eat, they have expert fish fryers to serve you perfect fish and chips and other excellent seafood dishes. Smart and slick and very clever indeed, Quinlan's is a model of how to serve fish and shellfish smartly and creatively. *The Mall, Tralee, County Kerry + 353 66 7123998. Open daily.*

The Roast House

They have their own on-site coffee roastery in the Roast House, set in the lovely terrace of Denny Street in the centre of town, so it's the place for that good cup of Java. But whilst the roasting may bring you in first, the good cooking will make you linger longer – homemade fishcake with citrus and chervil mayo; smoked salmon, leek and Gruyere quiche; salmon with green beans and chive cream; Mexican chicken with guacamole on toasted sourdough; fillet of beef with mushroom and Parmesan tart. And then a perfect cup of coffee to finish the treat. *3 Denny Street, Tralee, County Kerry + 353 66 7181011 www.theroasthouse.ie. Open daily, weekend dinner.*

Spa Seafoods

Spa Seafoods has the best fish cookery in this part of the country, along with simply amazing views over the Dingle peninsula from the upstairs dining room. It's a short journey out from Tralee, but it's a trip everyone is happy to make to enjoy fish cookery of this quality and creativity. If you just want a snack rather than a full meal, then there are stools and tables available downstairs where they can quickly rustle up a good a bowl of chowder, and the shop sells a superb range of really excellent artisan foods. *The Spa, Tralee, County Kerry + 353 66 7136901 www.spaseafoods.com. Open lunch & dinner.*

Craft Brewery

The **West Kerry Brewery** is Europe's most westerly micro-brewery, operating from Bric's Pub, on the Slea Head Drive. If ever a trio of beers deserved to have a sea salty tang to them, it's the coastal trio Béal Bán, the Cul Dorcha and the Carrig Dubh.

www.westkerrybrewery.ie

Above: Spa Seafoods

Local Spirit

The **Dingle Distillery** is the first distillery created to fashion a new whiskey to be purpose built in Ireland in 200 years. Owned by the dynamic Porterhouse Brewing Company of Dublin, the first spirit for the whiskey was laid down in December 2012. When it is ready, the whiskey will be a five year old, triple pot-stilled single malt. Believe it or not, but at one time there were 1,200 distilleries scattered throughout the island of Ireland. Today, like artisan beer making, which suffered a long decline in Ireland before coming back with astonishing vigour in the last five years, artisanal distilling is again dynamic, with some twenty applications for distilleries having been lodged in recent times. Meantime, whilst waiting for the Dingle whiskey, do try the fine Dingle Original Gin and Dingle pot still Vodka: they help to pass the time.

www.dingledistillery.ie

Louis Mulcahy, Caifé na Caolóige

Louis Mulcahy is one of Ireland's most famous potters and, like the man himself, there is artistic discrimination evident in everything the kitchen sends out, and it makes Caifé na Caolóige a vital destination on any Slea Head and Wild Atlantic Way tour. And when you consider that lots of the vegetables and leaves have come from no further than their own raised beds and other local plots and polytunnels, and most everything else is sourced from the peninsula, you know you are getting the true taste of the Dingle peninsula. If you can leave without buying a gorgeous piece of Mr Mulcahy's pottery, then you are made of sterner stuff than us. *Clogher Strand, Slea Head, County Kerry + 353 66 9156229 www.louismulcahy.com open day time.*

Gorman's Clifftop House

Quite how Vincent and Sile Gorman manage to maintain such a productive herb and vegetable garden, here in this guesthouse and restaurant at the edge of Smerwick Harbour, where the winds whirl and swirl endlessly, we don't quite know. But their fresh leaves and herbs add mightily to Vincent's classic cooking, bringing colour and contrast to the culinary canvas in Gorman's. Great comfort, great views. *Glaise Bheag, Ballydavid, Dingle, County Kerry + 353 66 9155162 www.gormans-clifftophouse.com. Open dinner.*

Right: John R's
Opposite: The Chart House

Ashe's Bar

A simple thing happens when you walk into Sinéad and Thomas's bar: you don't want to leave. You may have only come in for a quick drink or a quick bite to eat, but we'll bet you change your plans very fast, and have another drink, and another plate of something delicious. Sure, the night is young, and how often nowadays do you find yourself in a classic pub like Ashe's, a pub with that inimitable, out-of-time character, and with excellent cooking. Nice simple rooms upstairs also. *Main Street, Dingle, County Kerry + 353 66 9150989 www.ashesbar.ie. Open lunch & dinner.*

An Canteen

Brothers Niall and Brian are fastidious about their sourcing in An Canteen, so head here for seafood chowder, Dingle hake, braised Kerry lamb shoulder. Great value for money. *Dykegate Lane, Dingle, County Kerry + 353 86 6603778 www.ancanteen.com*

The Boatyard

It was a particularly brilliant crab quiche that first alerted our correspondent to the excellence of Caroline Danaher's restaurant, but when you discover that everything else is as good as that crab quiche, then you will know you have discovered a creative and dynamic seafood restaurant. Value for money is excellent. *Strand Street, Dingle, County Kerry + 353 66 9150920 www.theboatyardrestaurant.ie*

Castlewood

Just how much work does it take to maintain a house at the pitch-perfect level that Brian and Helen manage at Dingle's iconic Castlewood House? Every time you visit the house looks freshly painted: all of it! Everything gleams. The result is one of the best places to stay in Ireland, and one of the very best breakfasts, not just in Ireland but, we reckon, anywhere in the world. *The Wood, Dingle, County Kerry + 353 66 9152788 www.castlewooddingle.com*

Cookery School

The Dingle Cookery School

Mark Murphy and his team will not only teach you how to cook fish, they will take you out on a boat first and teach you how to catch fish. This sort of dynamic interactive thesis has seen the Dingle Cookery School burst into people's consciousness, so scan the DCS website before you head to Kerry and book in for a course that will raise your culinary standards sky high.

http://dinglecookeryschool.ie

⍟ Chart House

Charming is a word that doesn't suit many modern places to eat, but the Chart House is pure charm. This is due to the wonderful service, partly to the domestic nature of the design, partly to the fact that the cooking is graciously modest, whilst being never other than professionally precise. And, the vegetables they serve are out of this world: you won't taste a better spud in Kerry. *The Mall, Dingle, County Kerry + 353 66 915 2255 www.thecharthousedingle.com*

⍟ Dingle Reel Fish Co

Mark Grealy's fish and chip shop is one of the best in Ireland. The best fish from the harbour and the best, driest chips are delivered by a masterly cook who takes his calling seriously. Worth the drive to Dingle. *Holy Ground, Dingle, County Kerry + 353 66 915 1713. Open lunch and dinner.*

Above: Emlagh House
Below: The Chart House

🛏 Emlagh House

There is something extraordinarily gratifying about Emlagh. It's a place where everything conspires to gratify your senses - the tactility of the tableware, the sweep of the dining room windows and their view out onto Dingle Bay, the gorgeous art works that dot the house. It's a house that spells comfort, as you help yourself to a DOG (Dingle Original Gin) and tonic and sink into a mercilessly comfortable armchair. The cooking amplifies this feel-good factor, with beautifully realised breads and egg dishes, superb French toast, robust bacon and sausages from Ashe's of Annascaul, all perfectly executed. Each time you come back it's where you want to be and, for many people, in a town with fine standards, Emlagh is the only place. *Dingle, County Kerry + 353 66 9152345 www.emlaghhouse.com*

Fish at the Marina

OK, so I'm having the legendary seared tuna burger with black olive relish and chips, but I also want a taste of salt 'n' pepper chilli squid. You're having the organic salmon fillet with gnocchi, spinach, tomato and basil, but you also want to try the classic calamari. Now, that's a dilemma, but aren't we having a lovely time here in Alex Barr's place on the Marina. *Marina Buildings, Dingle, County Kerry + 353 86 378 8584. Open day time.*

Global Village

Talk to culinary professionals and talk to culinary critics and you will discover that both of them rate Martin Bealin's cooking in Global Village as being right at the top of the tree. Mr Bealin has been at the stoves a long time, but there is youth in his food, and he sources ingredients with a meticulousness that is inspiring. The room is beautiful, service is calm and gracious and, as one starry chef put it, "I was just blown away by the cooking!" If you want to know how Dingle climbed to the top of the food barometer, then dinner here will show you a standard setter for the town that laid down the parameters and principles which everyone else set out to match. Not just a great Kerry restaurant, but a great European restaurant. *Upper Main Street, Dingle, County Kerry + 353 66 915 2325 www.globalvillage.com. Open dinner.*

Local Food

Jerry Kennedy is one of the pre-eminent Irish butchers, a master of the craft whose skills with rearing, sourcing and preparing meats underpin the food culture of the town. Mr Kennedy is particularly known for offering lamb reared on the Blasket Islands, where the shepherd is Donncha O'Ceileachair and where, as Donncha says, "the sheep are grazing on land that was never ploughed, so there is a nice mixture of grassland and heather." The **Blasket lamb** is unique, but so is the Dingle Peninsula lamb which Jerry sources from a network of farms on the peninsula, and equally superb is the beef from Jerry's own farm. It's all great.

⫶ Goat Street Bistro

'Slow food and fast service'. Can there be a higher aspiration in the world of food than to achieve those twin aims? But that is what Ed and Laurence achieve in the funky Goat Street Bistro, and they do it in a splendidly personal way. Customers tend to use expressions like 'new age' or 'could be in San Francisco' to describe the ambience and the creatively atypical cooking of the GSB. But, in fact, when you think about it, it's pure Dingle, pure West Kerry: people doing things according to their philosophies and their culinary culture, and doing it as well as they possibly can. *Main Street, Dingle, County Kerry + 353 66 915 2770 www.goatstreetcafe.com Open lunch & dinner.*

Local Food

Kerry, and Dingle in particular have a long tradition of making pies. **Piog Pies**, in Dingle carry on the tradition with a wonderful array of pastries available throughout the peninsula. Look out for them in local shops and markets.

🛏 Greenmount

The Curran family have been beacons of hospitality since they opened Greenmount in 1977, and if you ask anyone who has stayed in the family's house to explain the appeal of this Dingle icon, you are likely to be told that it is the handmade nature of so much of what they do. Breakfast, with its fresh handmade breads, lovely handmade preserves, delectable poached fruits, and freshly cooked hot dishes, is a masterclass in the art. *Upper John Street, Dingle, County Kerry + 353 66 9151414 www.greenmounthouse.ie*

🛏 Heatons

Cameron, Nuala and David Heaton seem able to read their guests' minds, so you will have scarcely made a request for something or other before they have it sorted. Their hospitality is only mighty, and the water's edge location is perfect. *The Wood, Dingle, County Kerry + 353 66 9152288 www.heatonsdingle.com*

Idás

Kevin Murphy's cooking in Idás is delicate and re-fined, but it's also focused and grounded, and several of the Idás menu dishes are already signature dishes that underpin his menus – scallop with pig's cheek and pommes Anna; beef cheek and rib-eye steak with mushroom duxelles; poached lobster tail with crisp pork belly and broad bean hash; hake fillets with crab-bouleh. As befits a guy who originally trained as an artist, the food is painterly and picture perfect on the plate, and the room itself is quite lovely. Idás is a most harmonious restaurant, and Mr Murphy's first year in Dingle town has been met with unanimous acclaim.
The Bull's Head, John Street, Dingle, County Kerry + 353 83 1036973

Opposite: Maja Binder at the Little Cheese Shop
Below: On The Wild Side

The Little Cheese Shop

Maja Binder is a cheesemaker who also runs a cheese shop: now, that's being qualified for your job. TLCS is a wonderful place to find wonderful cheeses in mint condition, as well as great foods and – hungry traveller alert! – some really crackingly desirable sandwiches for lunch. Don't miss this Dingle gem.
Grey's Lane, Dingle, County Kerry + 353 87 6255788 www.thelittlecheeseshop. net

Milltown House

Long before Dingle transformed itself into one of the brightest and best places to eat and stay in Ireland, Milltown House was here, offering serene hospitality and heartbreakingly gorgeous views across the bay. Today, under the guidance of Stephen McPhilemy and Patrick Wade, the house has undergone a beautiful re-birth, and stands once again as one of the defining Dingle addresses. Right from the moment you arrive, and have your first encounter with Seamus, the formidable wolfhound (who runs the place, of course) Milltown strikes the right notes of hospitality, generosity and fun. *Milltown, Dingle, County Kerry + 353 83 1477363 www.milltownhouse.com*

Murphy's Ice Cream

The original Murphy's ice cream store in Dingle remains a place with a unique ambience, and it has been one of the pivotal players in the culinary renaissance of Dingle that has seen the town rocket to pre-eminence, in particular when their annual food festival takes over the entire town in October. To say that the Murphy brothers make ice cream is to say that Horowitz played the piano. Better to say that they express their creativity, via the medium of ice cream. The coffees are amazing also, and the staff are as good as it gets. *Strand Street, Dingle, County Kerry + 353 66 9152644 www.murphysicecream.ie*

Out of the Blue

A funny thing happens in OOTB. Staff come, and then they go, and then they come back, back to that special place that has a special place in their heart: Out Of The Blue. In this sense, OOTB functions a bit like a family and, like a family, there is always a sense of organic progression, of maturing, of people coming back to the table with the fruits of what they have learnt. Happily, these fruits are there for the eating, and OOTB is one of the best seafood restaurants in Europe, with a delightful series of riffs on classic dishes: red mullet salad with onion compote;

their classic pollock in potato scale crust; john dory and sea bass with polenta; scallops with beurre blanc. The room – and the experience – is wonderfully colourful and vivid, the wines are blissful, and all is good. *Waterside, Dingle, County Kerry + 353 66 9150811 www.outoftheblue.ie. Open lunch and dinner.*

Pax House
John O'Farrell could have called his house Sea View, because the views from the sea facing side of the house and from the patio are stupendous. Four new rooms with views have been created during the winter, making the house even more sumptuous. *Upper John St, Dingle, County Kerry + 353 66 9151518 www. pax-house.com*

The Phoenix
'Rising from the side of a busy road just beyond Inch beach, is the wonderland that is Lorna Tyther's baby. Pull in and park your car and you'll soon forget about everything in the outside world.' That's the sort of instant effect Lorna and Billy Tyther's vegetarian guesthouse and restaurant, The Phoenix, tends to have on people. You pitch up here and the world vanishes. In its place arises The Phoenix, a quixotic demi-monde of inspired vegetarian cooking, belly-dancing and hippy-dippy hard work from the proprietors that ensures you will have a wonderful time. *Shanahill East, Castlemaine, County Kerry + 353 66 9766284 www. thephoenixrestaurant.ie*

Milltown Market
Mary O'Riordan's Organic Store is a one-stop-organic supermarket. Everything you need is here, from the best local organic vegetables to wines to cheeses to fruits to books and including smashing gardening gear from the best specialists in Ireland. And as you would expect from an idealistic and community-minded person, prices in Mary's Organic Store are very keen indeed. *Milltown, County Kerry + 353 66 9767869 www.milltownorganicstore.com*

Above: Out of the Blue
Opposite: The South Pole Inn

10
The Ring
of Kerry

The most singular thing about Kerry, aside perhaps from the confident but not unpleasing pride of the locals, is the character of the light that washes over the county. At times it can seem to be purest monochrome, with sheets of celluloid silver light dissecting the hob-black tones that cover the hills. Then, with a sweep of wind that is announced by a cannon-fire rumble through the valleys, it will change to become peat-dark and gun-metal grey, and the hills will appear to be backlit, like some stage set or a post-modern painted landscape. The sea will dance with threatening dark washes devoid of colour, a lick of white foam fringing the waves, whilst on the land the light will fade to softer, natural shades.

It is an uncanny theatre of non-colours, and you try to explain away the curiousness of it all by reference to how far west the county is slung, how deeply sunk in the Atlantic ocean so much of it is. But this won't somehow convince you that the weird and singular quality of the light isn't just another aspect of the mysticism which can seem so readily believable in County Kerry. The soft mists with the promising threat of what hides behind them, the swirling fogs that further inoculate the light, the sense that a prospect of simple abandonment could lie just around the corner. You might find yourself here and just decide to stay, simple as that.

WILD
ATLANTIC
WAY

Valentia Ice-cream

Unhomogenised milk, buttermilk, yogurts with fruit, sorbets and numerous varieties of ice cream are the proud products that Joe and Caroline Daly make from the milk of their herd of friesians. It would be hard to better the quality of milk from a herd grazing on these windswept, sea salt spattered pastures. The milk and ice creams are pure tasting and delicious, and one senses that a search for purity – they wisely disdain homogenisation, for example – is what animates the Dalys. Don't miss their lovely dairy products, and do try to find the time to visit the ice cream booth at the farm itself.

www.valentiadairy.com

Ard na Sidhe

It's been one of the dishes of the year. If you had the good fortune to stay at the gorgeous Ard na Sidhe, a very, very precise and perfect rendition of the Arts & Crafts style of design which is very rare in Ireland, and you then ordered a starter dish of twice-baked crab soufflé with hazelnut crust served with a shell-fish and tomato bisque, then you hit the jackpot twice – a gorgeous destination, and one of the great dishes of the year.'One of the best dishes we tasted', said our man, Eugene, and in 2014 lots of others agreed. Chef Dylan Kelly and manageress Jennifer Dowling are creating a magical experience here at the edge of Caragh Lake, and if the hotel is postcard-perfect, the setting is equally idyllic. Mr Kelly's expertise isn't just confined to his iconic starter, however: his cooking is fluent throughout the concise and well-chosen menus that showcase local lamb and beef and fine fish and shellfish. The house itself is simply drop-dead gorgeous, having been meticulously restored before its re-opening, and Ard na Sidhe is on a roll. *Caragh Lake, Killorglin, County Kerry + 353 66 9769105 www.ardnasidhe.com*

Nick's

Nick's is a step back in time, to the time of red banquettes, white tablecloths, carpets and fireplaces, bentwood chairs and kindly ladies in charge of service. For which we say: Hurrah! So, decide whether you want to eat in the bar or the restaurant, then order up the classics – prawn and monkfish thermidor; grilled lobster; rack of Kerry lamb with fondant potato; Dover sole with lemon butter sauce. *Lwr Bridge Street, Killorglin, County Kerry + 353 66 9761219. www.nicks.ie. Open dinner.*

Sol y Sombra

A tapas bar and music venue in a deconsecrated Church of Ireland? Only in Kerry, that's for sure. Cliodhna Foley's inspired adventure is so off the wall that it takes your breath away. You can even have your wedding reception here: now, what a day that would be! But, even if you haven't popped the question, the foods and wines in Sol y Sombra are reason to come here, and return here – bacon and egg bechamel croquettes; suckling pig; sausage with apple marmalade – and don't miss the wonderful sherries. *The Old Church of Ireland, Killorglin, County Kerry + 353 66 9762357 www.solysombra.ie. Open dinner.*

Zest Café

Nicola Foley's Zest Café is a pulsing and integral part of the Foley family's trio of establishments, a stylish and happening room where it seems that every dish they offer, from breakfast to brunch to lunch and into the afternoon, somehow has your name on it. Value and service chime sweetly with every other detail of a café that gives us zest for living. *School Road, Killorglin, County Kerry + 353 66 979 0303 www.zestcafe.ie. Open day time.*

Jack's

Jack and Celine have everything you need in their super emporium, and the shelves here are positively groaning with breads, cakes and superb deli foods. *Lower Bridge Street, Killorglin, County Kerry + 353 66 976 1132. Open day time.*

Jack's Coastguard Restaurant

Jack's is an icon in and around Cromane, a sure-fire success story for beautifully cooked seafood served in a lovely room with a superlative location. The Keary family really do their best to look after everyone. Just make sure to get there early for Sunday lunch. *Cromane, County Kerry + 353 66 9769102 www.jackscromane.com. Open lunch and dinner.*

Local Food

Sneem Black Pudding

Sneem is a tiny village which manages to boast not just one handmade Kerry black pudding, but two. You will find them in O'Sullivan's butcher's, and in Burns' family butcher's. Buy both to compare and contrast, and remember that black pudding is cooked and is best if heated in the oven, rather than fried in a frying pan.

⍾ Petit Delice

You don't really expect to find a French bakery and tea rooms on the Ring of Kerry, but here it is: Petit Delice is bakery, lunch time destination, ice cream stop, chocolate fix and coffee stop! 'You can imagine that you are deep in La France Profonde', said the *FT*. There is a second branch in Killarney. *Cahirciveen, County Kerry + 353 87 9903572*

⍾ O'Neill's The Point Bar

Michael and Bridie O'Neill source their fish from Quinlan's fish shops for their fish and shellfish menu, and the cooking is lip smackin' simple and tasty. Make sure to get here early – it's a very busy spot – to enjoy spankingly fresh seafood in a charming, family-run pub. *Renard Point, Cahirciveen, County Kerry + 353 66 9472165 Open lunch & dinner in season.*

🛏 QCs

Kate and Andrew Cooke added the most stunningly stylish series of rooms to their fine restaurant a few years back, and instantly established QC's as the hippest destination on the Ring of Kerry. Eddie Gannon's cooking in the restaurant follows the design ethos of QC's: take top-class materials, and treat them with empathy and respect, imagination and creativity. *3 Main Street, Caherciveen, County Kerry + 353 66 9472244 www.qcbar.com. Open lunch and dinner.*

🛏 The Moorings

Pan-fried hake with Gubbeen chorizo mash and lemon butter. Isn't that just the sort of lip smackin' dinner dish that the hungry traveller wants to find set before him, after a long day's journeying out and back to the Skelligs? Indeed it is, and it's just the sort of thing Patricia and Gerard will set before you in The Moorings. Mr and Mrs Kennedy have made the Moorings a little world unto itself, with the restaurant, bar, gift shop, guest rooms and a self-catering cottage. *Portmagee, County Kerry + 353 66 9477108 Open lunch & dinner.*

Iskeroon

Iskeroon's extraordinary location at the ocean's edge explains its world-wide renown as a unique place to stay, and David and Geraldine have designed and furnished the suites and self-catering apartment with just the right sort of chic rusticity. Iskeroon is unforgettable, not least the drive down the winding road and then across the beach to the house. *Caherdaniel, County Kerry + 353 66 9475119 www.iskeroon.com.*

Parknasilla

"A brilliant place to stay" was how one of our correspondents summed up his few days relaxing at the legendary Parknasilla. In particular, he singled out the skills of John Foley, the restaurant manager at Parknasilla, as someone right on top of his game. The location of the hotel is breathtaking, the grounds are magnificent, and you will find it very hard to leave this little bit of paradise when the time comes to depart. *Sneem, County Kerry + 353 64 667 5600 www.parknasillaresort.com*

The Boathouse

This stylish waterside restaurant is owned and run by the smart people behind The Park Hotel, Kenmare. A pretty relaxed space, only yards from the sea. *Dromquinna Estate, Kenmare, County Kerry + 353 64 6642889 Open lunch and dinner.*

Drumquinna Manor Glamping

Whilst the main house at John Brennan's Dromquinna Manor is reserved for weddings and events, it is the luxury glamping in the beautiful grounds of the Manor that are of most interest to travellers on the WAW. Banish any thoughts of camping hardship – this is 5-star camping in superbly comfortable, specially-designed tents, and then there is The Boathouse Bistro on site to tempt you with tasty food and a superlative menu of specialist gins. *Drumquinna Estate, Kenmare, County Kerry + 353 64 6642888 www.dromquinnamanor.com/luxury-camping.html*

Below: Drumquinna Manor

Brook Lane

The Brook Lane Hotel offers exactly what you want, without pretension, without silliness, without nonsense, and it shows a team who care about the small details, whether it is how to furnish a room, orchestrate your weekend or your wedding, or how to make a perfect fish pie. Despite their relative youth, Dermot and Una Brennan have mature heads on their shoulders, and we love the way they do their thing. They are true hoteliers, alive to every nuance of the profession, always getting better. *Kenmare, County Kerry + 353 64 6642077 www.brooklanehotel.com.*

Hawthorn House

Mary and Noel run a cosy, comfy, welcoming B&B right in the centre of Kenmare, and it's a perfect base for exploring the culinary charms of Kenmare and for relaxing after a day on the WAW. *Shelbourne Street, Kenmare, County Kerry + 353 64 6641035.*

Jam

The staff in Jam, a comfy, cosy café are so good, so charming, so friendly, that were they to tell us that they had nothing but cheese strings and gruel to offer, we would sit down and have cheese strings and gruel. Thankfully, they offer smashing proper food, and the place is always packed. *6 Henry Street, Kenmare, County Kerry + 353 64 6641591. Open day time.*

Below: The Park Hotel

The Lime Tree

Mike Casey has returned to his early stomping ground in the beautiful Lime Tree restaurant, one of Kenmare's prettiest rooms. Right from the off he married classic-era cooking – Sneem pudding with apple compote; duo of Kerry lamb; Hereford beef with green peppercorn sauce; Skeaghanore duck with cassis sauce; Lime Tree crepes – with excellent service and good value. As we write, Mr Casey is also planning to open a deli venture in the centre of Kenmare. *Shelburne Street, Kenmare, County Kerry + 353 64 6641225 www.limetreerestaurant.com*

Mulcahy's

Quietly, surely, confidently, whilst everyone was looking somewhere else, Bruce Mulcahy climbed to the top of the culinary tree in Ireland. It's where he belongs, and his confidence today means he inhabits the lofty space comfortably, rubbing shoulders with the best. His cooking is vivid and fun: his veal cheek ravioli would thrill you if you ate it in a Ligurian enoteca. His beef tartare with tarragon purée and toasted sourdough would make Fernand Point smile, before M. Point wolfed down the plate. The attention to detail is microscopic, the success is massive. Great value for money, too. *Market Street, Kenmare, County Kerry + 353 64 6642383. Open dinner.*

No 35

Dermot and Una Brennan run restaurant No 35 as well as the lovely Brook Lane Hotel, and you will see the same fastidious creativity here in the centre of town in a charming restaurant. The food sourcing is meticulous and in particular don't miss their own rare-breed pork. *Main Street, Kenmare, County Kerry + 353 64 6641559. Open dinner.*

Packie's

Martin Hallisey's cooking in Packie's, one of the legendary Kenmare addresses, is neither modern nor traditional, though it has elements of both. Truthfully, it's food that is outside of fashion, and outside of time, so you might have roast duck, or Irish stew, or cod Provencale or seafood sausage with beurre blanc and it will all be delicious. Service is as genial as the chef and his food. One of the Kenmare standard bearers. *Henry Street, Kenmare, County Kerry + 353 64 6641508. Open dinner.*

Park Hotel

If you think that polished, practiced hospitality has little or no place in our modern, informal world, then come to Francis and John Brennan's legendary hotel, The Park, and you will find that polished, practiced hospitality is alive and well. What's more, you will discover that doing things correctly is infinitely pleasing, and that it is in no way anachronistic in our modern, informal world. Hospitality this good exists outside of time or fashion. *Kenmare, County Kerry + 353 64 664 1200 www.parkkenmare.com*

Purple Heather

Grainne O'Connell is one of the select band of Kenmare Food Heroes, people who not only carved out the town's reputation for good food, but who also maintain it, day after day, through sheer hard work. Something about the room always makes us yearn for classic food when we are here – chicken liver pâté with Cumberland sauce, the mushroom omelette, the cheese platter, the seafood pie. Class. *Henry Street, Kenmare, County Kerry + 353 64 6641016*

Shelburne Lodge

Shelburne Lodge is one of the most beautiful places to stay in Ireland. Having distinguished herself as one of Kenmare's greatest cooks when she ran restaurants down in the town, in Shelburne Maura Foley shows herself to be one of the great designers, decorators, and hosts. Shelburne Lodge is sublime in every detail: the design, the decoration, the artworks and – most especially – the breakfasts, which are the stuff of legend.

Tom looks after everyone as if he was your favourite uncle. *Killowen, Kenmare, County Kerry + 353 64 6641013 www.shelburnelodge.com*

Local Food

Kenmare Select are a specialist salmon smoking company. Their distinctive fish is uniquely sold in full-length, razor-thin slices to restaurants and chefs throughout Europe. Good news for WAW travellers is that you can also buy it locally in shops around Kenmare. Order it whenever you see it!

www.kenmare-select.com

Opposite & Centre: Mulcahy's Restaurant

Opposite: Shelburne Lodge flowers

Local Food

Kerry boasts a number of small chocolate factories in unlikely locations. Way out in Ballinskelligs you will find the **Skelligs Chocolate Company** beside the **Cocoa Bean Artisan Chocolates.** These two gifted artisan chocolate companies work side-by-side at St Finian's Bay. You are welcome to visit the factory, they give regular tours. Meanwhile further inland, French chocolatier Benoit Lorge works out of an old post office by the side of the road in Bonane making the prized **Lorge Chocolates.**

www.skelligschocolate.com
www.lorgechocolate.com

Sailors Bar

Our copy editor, Judith Casey, first introduced us to the Sailor's Bar, a no-nonsense pit stop just west of Kenmare that serves good fish and simple suppers in an amiable, informal setting. Aha! Just the sort of place you want to find while travelling the Wild Atlantic Way. *Castletownbere Road, Kenmare, County Kerry + 353 64 6642684*

Vanilla Grape

Alain Bras stocks an idiosyncratic, intriguing selection of wines in this cute shop. Originally a sommelier and wine lecturer of considerable renown, M. Bras culls wines from 35 regions for his shelves, and the selection is distinguished by his in-depth knowledge of the entire world of wine. *12 Henry Street, Kenmare, County Kerry + 353 64 6640694 www.alainbras.com.*

Wharton's

There are droves of people who will argue vehemently with you should you dare to suggest that there is a better chipper than Wharton's of Kenmare. They will be joined by the massed citizens of Kenmare, who cherish their famous fish and chip shop, a place where everything is made from scratch and cooked to order. Ace grub, and smashing staff. *Main Street, Kenmare, County Kerry + 353 64 6642622 www.whartonskenmare.com. Open lunch and dinner.*

Josie's Lakeview House Restaurant

Josie's is the last stop in County Kerry and here you will find simple cooking, terrific views of Glanmore Lake, a bed and breakfast apartment and even a self-catering cottage if you feel like getting to know the area better. The lunchtime offer is soups, salads and sandwiches, with a more extensive assortment of fish dishes and rack of lamb and steaks in the evening, and plenty of good vegetables. It's fun, it's remote, and there is generosity evident everywhere. *Lauragh, County Kerry + 353 64 6683155 www.josiesrestaurant.ie Open lunch and dinner.*

11
The Ring
of Beara

The Beara Peninsula is where Irish artisan food production was reignited. Sometime around about 1976, way down south on the rugged Beara, in farthest, deepest West Cork, Veronica and Norman Steele, who had three cows on their little farm, "started making cheese as a way of stashing milk for the winter".

The Steeles called their cheese Milleens, and it was a washed-rind, semi-soft cheese made with raw milk. Those were the only aspects of Milleens that were conventional, however. In terms of flavour and texture, Milleens was unlike anything being made by anyone else anywhere else. Milleens was a mighty template of tastes, with floral, sweet, mushroomy, resinous flavour notes all bundled up in its carefully, hand-washed rind.

It was a cheese that was both earthy and ethereal, and it created the signature style for all the Irish farmhouse cheeses that quickly followed its example: when your cheese expressed the singular place from which it originated, then you had made a successful cheese.

Milleens spoke of West Cork. It spoke of Beara, of the cow in the field on the sea-surrounded peninsula.

WILD
ATLANTIC
WAY

Local Food

'It's basically a recipe' says Michael O'Neill on the process of making **Irish Atlantic Sea Salt.** The O'Neills create crisp flakes of snow-white salt that are slightly moist, flaky and crumble nicely when you crush them between your fingers. This is an artisan ingredient that has seen no refinement or additives, and consequently is a treasure of the region, with its own special taste.

www.irishatlanticsalt.ie

Harrington's

Come to Harrington's to enjoy a coffee in the café in the morning or a sandwich at lunchtime, sit outside at a table in the summer, then choose a nice bottle of wine to bring home. *Ardgroom, County Cork + 353 27 74003. Open day time until early evening.*

Rhonwen's Eateries Bistro

Who wouldn't go all the way to Eyeries to eat Rhonwen's Beara Buffalo Burger, local buffalo meat, served on a home-made bap, with a slice of the iconic Milleens cheese, hand-sliced slaw and hand-cut chips? Little travellers will want their own Gruffalo Burger, from a smart selection. A commitment to using local artisan foods and a family-run vibe is the style of Rhonwen's. *Eyeries, County Cork +353 27 74884. Open lunch and dinner.*

Dursey Deli

The Dursey Deli is the original food cart! It's essentially a chipper on wheels, but if you're lucky there'll be fresh mackerel from Dursey's beautiful bay. Time your trip on the cable car to coincide with lunch, and keep your fingers crossed for that mackerel. *Dursey, County Cork + 353 86 1799270. Open day time, seasonally.*

Berehaven Lodge

Berehaven Lodge is a handsome collection of self-catering lodges, three miles outside town, and of particular interest to travellers on the WAW is their Roan Carrig restaurant. The speciality is seafood – smoked cod Scotch egg; turbot with samphire and pease pudding; cod with cauliflower purée and truffle oil. There are good wines, craft beers, and views to die for. *Castletownbere, County Cork + 353 27 71464 www.berehavenholidayresort.ie*

Copper Kettle

The Copper Kettle is a modest space, specialising in enormous breakfasts. *Castletownbere, County Cork + 353 27 71792. Open day time.*

Loop de Loop

A key stop in Castletownbere, this handsome eco emporium sells wholesome foods. *Bank Place, Castletownbere, County Cork + 353 27 70770*

McCarthy's Bar

McCarthy's Bar is special. 'It might just be the best pub in the world', wrote the late Pete McCarthy. Pete was all too right. Be sure to ask Adrienne the story of her father Aidan's life. She will refer you to Aidan's book, which tells the incredible story of his wartime service. Once you open it, you won't be able to put it down. *The Square, Castletownbere, County Cork + 353 27 70014. Food served day time.*

Taste

Sheila Power's shop is simply jammers with good things — brilliant breads, organic vegetables, coffee, cheeses, wholefoods, wines, whatever you might need or could need. *Bank Place, Castletownbere, County Cork + 353 27 71943.*

Dromagowlane House

Anne and Paul grown their own foods on their 20 organic acres, so you can enjoy the real tastes of Beara here at breakfast time, and the fact that they cook evening meals by arrangement is really valuable, so bring on the fresh crab cakes, the beef and Guinness pie and the West Cork apple cake. *Adrigole, County Cork + 353 27 60330 www.dromagowlanehouse.com*

Peg's Shop

Maureen Sullivan runs a lovely shop here in Peg's. Like the best Beara stores, it's friendly, atmospheric and fun, with lots of tasty things to eat and good bottles of wine. *Adrigole, County Cork + 353 27 60007.*

12
Bantry Bay to the Sheep's Head

The Sheep's Head peninsula has always been the sleeper peninsula in West Cork, not as well-known as the Mizen, often overlooked in favour of the Beara. But a quiet renaissance has been taking place here in recent times, spurred initially by the Sheep's Head Way – which actually runs, or should we say, walks, all the way to Gougane Barra – and by the collective actions of the Sheep's Head producers group.

Today there is a critical cluster of food people and food places on the peninsula, unified by high standards and a creative imagination. And if you are persuaded to stay and linger awhile whilst travelling the WAW, by the B&B's and restaurants, then you will discover a very special, very quiet place, a place for walking, cycling, swimming, hiking. The Sheep's Head is a place that seems to attract unlikely people, who then do unlikely things there. And the great exemplar in this regard is Jeffa Gill, who has made Durrus Farmhouse Cheese, way, way up at the top of the hill of Coomken, for more than thirty years. We don't know if Ms Gill ever asked an accountant if it was a good business idea to make a raw milk cheese at the top of a remote hill on a remote peninsula: we suspect she didn't.

WILD ATLANTIC WAY

Opposite: Good Things Café

🛏 Bay View

The Bay View is a valuable stop both for its pretty tea rooms and also for some stylish accommodation, just south of Glengarriff. *Reenmeen, Glengarriff, County Cork + 353 27 63030 www.thebayviewboutiqueguesthouse.com.*

Local Food

West Cork is the home of Irish farmhouse cheese, with the pioneering semi-soft cheeses from **Milleens, Durrus** and **Gubbeen,** all of them pioneer cheeses, and all of them made by mighty women – Veronica Steele, Jeffa Gill, and Giana Ferguson. Someone needs to write that Ph.D thesis on what these women have achieved for Irish food, and for Irish feminism, and for Irish farming.

🍴 Dan Phils Restaurant

Christophe Zelliox has earned a great name for his cooking in various destinations in West Cork, so this new venture by the O'Sullivan family in the Ouvane Falls hotel bodes well. Sharon O'Sullivan leads the team out front, while M. Zelliox heads up the kitchen The views of the Ouvane river from the garden and dining room are pretty spectacular. *Ballylickey, Bantry, County Cork + 353 27 50056*

🛏 Eagle Point Camping

Eagle Point is one of the best campsites on the WAW. Its location, hard by the bay at Ballylickey, draws the same people back year after year, people who want to park the camper and pitch the tent in this little slice of West Cork heaven. Cronin's shop, at the filling station just across the road from the entrance, is a really excellent general store.

🍴 Manning's Emporium

Manning's is the West Cork space where everyone wants to be. As *McKennas' Guides* editor Eamon Barrett perfectly expressed it: 'Had a gang of friends down in Durrus for the weekend doing all the touristy things - Garinish, Mizen Head... the weather was fantastic and West Cork delivered its special kind of magic to these first time visitors and everyone had a great time. Manning's was out the door busy - something which gives me great joy to see.' Manning's is pretty much always out-the-door busy, simply

because Laura, Andrew and Val serve lovely foods, create a wonderful atmosphere, and give everyone a taste of West Cork à la mer. There is no other food space like Manning's, and its dynamic present is a wonderful echo of its essential and distinguished past. *Ballylickey, County Cork + 353 27 50456 www.manningsemporium.ie. Open day time.*

Sea View House Hotel

Kathleen O'Sullivan's beautiful hotel in Ballylickey is the favourite West Cork destination for very many very discriminating people. Ms O'Sullivan runs her hotel the old school way, with correct cooking, correct service, simple and correct design, eager and correct housekeeping. As a guest, the pleasures to be derived from her didactic approach to running an hotel are myriad, and you find yourself saying 'Why aren't there more hotels like this, places where nothing is too much trouble, places where they look after you?' And look after you is what they do in the Sea View House Hotel. *Ballylickey, County Cork + 353 27 50073 www.seaviewhousehotel.com*

Below: Dexter beef. Sold in Mannings.

Bantry Market

You will find us in Bantry Market on Friday mornings, hunting down the Toonsbridge burrata, the Maughnasilly eggs, the Wok About stir-fries, the organic vegetables and the Gubbeen pork, the West Cork pies and the O'Driscoll's fish, before we have a slice of Base pizza or maybe something tasty from Frankie's BBQ. Wolfe Tone Square, Bantry, County Cork. Fridays.

 Eden Crest

Josephine and Barry have been offering West Cork hospitality to visitors to Eden Crest for twenty years now. The house has a perfect location – a couple of minutes west of Bantry town on the N71 – and is a great base for exploring West Cork and Kerry. The house is comfy and welcoming, breakfasts are wholesome and tasty, and what stands out is the attention to detail. *Glengarriff Road, Bantry, County Cork + 353 27 51110 www.bantrybandb.com*

Fish Kitchen

Ann Marie's Fish Kitchen is upstairs above the fish shop, and it's a charming room in which to enjoy excellent fish and shellfish cookery right in the centre of town. Great service, and great value for money, means the Fish Kitchen really ticks all the boxes. *New Street, Bantry, County Cork + 353 27 56651 www. thefishkitchen.ie. Open lunch and dinner.*

Right: Martin O'Flynn, Maughnasily Farm, in the Bantry Market

Ma Murphys

Ma Murphy's is a wonderfully authentic Irish pub, a warren of cosy, intimate rooms where it's easy – all too easy – to lose a few hours with the perfect bottle of craft beer or two. Sean and Mary and their excellent staff ensure the bar is always inviting, and visitors to the town should not miss this classic West Cork pub, which offers the best range of Irish craft beers that you will find locally. *New Street, Bantry, County Cork + 353 27 50242*

Organico

Hannah and Rachel Dare are at the very centre of West Cork's unique food culture. They inhabit it, they define it, they practice it, and they preach it. In Organico, the shop, and Organico, the café, they give a masterclass in what the West Cork food culture is – original, unclichéd, unexpected, soulful, sophisticated, delicious. They exemplify the Zen restlessness that drives the food culture, so whilst they are forever seeking to improve what they do, forever looking to learn, to get better, their search is conducted in a calm, serene manner: they develop, and they do so organically. Stepping into Organico is like stepping out of the real world, into a pair of spaces that feel natural and instinctual, places that feel just right, that make you feel instantly better. One of the great Irish cafés and shops, and not to be missed by any visitor. *Glengarriff Road, Bantry, County Cork + 353 27 51391 www.organico.ie. Open day time.*

Whartons

Wharton's are serious about their fish and chips. Where other chippers heat pre-cooked fish and chips, they make everything from scratch here when you place your order – the potatoes are sent through the chipper, then placed in the deep-fryer, and the fish is readied. It makes for excellent eating, and the room is always pristine and beautifully maintained. Even the vinegar is carefully chosen! A benchmark chipper. *New Street, Bantry, County Cork*

¶ The Snug

The Snug isn't trendy. It's a classic traditional West Cork pub, and that is precisely what everyone likes about it. Maurice and Colette take care of things: he cooks the delicious food, she minds the bar and the customers, and they both do a superb job. So, pull up a stool at the counter – that's if you can get a seat as it's always jammers in here – and order plaice with mushroom sauce, a good cheese burger, West Cork sirloin and gravy, baked haddock, minute steak, and relish the amazing vegetables. Heartwarming, delicious and delightful, and sure let's have another pint, what do you say? *The Quay, Bantry, County Cork + 353 27 50057. Open lunch and dinner.*

¶ Stuffed Olive

Here's the kind of cook Trish Messom of The Stuffed Olive is: she will discover something delicious while on a trip, and then she will bring the idea back to Bantry and work on it until she has mastered it, and improved it. She is one of the defining culinary autodidacts, always learning, polishing, perfecting. She is devoted to the foods of West Cork, the foods whose tastes defined her childhood, and so she sources everything locally, and shows it respect and attention. She is one of those rare cooks whose every culinary gesture creates an archetype. Her cakes are dreamscapes. Her savoury cooking is ruddy and real. Her salads

shout: goodness! Her drinks are narcotic. Her traditional lamb stew would sustain the nation. All this, and you also get terrific service from Trish's daughters, Sarah and Grace, and the sort of vivid, vibrant ambience in the room that pulls you in off the street. A true star of Bantry, no doubt about it. *Bridge Street, Bantry, County Cork + 353 27 55883. Open day time.*

Bank House Restaurant on Whiddy Island
Staying here is both restorative and exciting, from quiet freshwater fishing to adventurous sea fishing. The family also run the local ferry. *Whiddy Island, County Cork + 353 86 8626734 www.whiddyferry.com*

Drumcloc House B&B
Swim or fish from their shoreline at Drumcloc, and enjoy good West Cork hospitality. There is a tennis court and a peaceful garden. *Bantry, County Cork + 353 27 50030 www.dromclochouse.com.*

Bernie's Cupán Tae Café
At the end of the Sheep's Head Way, at the end of Europe, there is a cup of tea, and a salmon sandwich, that have your name on them. If you have hiked down to Tooreen, with the lighthouse as your destination, then the tea and the sandwich waiting for you in Bernie Tobin's tea room will taste like the greatest thing you have ever eaten in your entire life. *Toreen Car Park, Sheep's Head, County Cork + 353 27 67878*

Above: Maurice and Colette from The Snug

Opposite: Trish Messom from The Stuffed Olive

🍴 Eileen's Bar

Eileen's is a gorgeous pub. Perfect after a hike around the Sheep's Head, for sitting by the fire, drinking glasses of hot port and pints of porter. The atmosphere is always great, and there are nice things to eat: a classic of the genre. *Fitzpatrick's Pub, Kilcrohane, County Cork + 353 27 67057*

🍴 Sheep's Head Producers Shop Restaurant & Market

West Cork is known to be a place where artists, crafts people and food lovers have chosen to live, and that's what makes this collaborative enterprise so special. There is a shop, selling local foods and a regular market. It's exciting, and it's terrific fun, so come along and meet everyone. *The Old Creamery, Kilcrohane, County Cork + 353 86 303 0991 https://sheepshead-market.wordpress.com*

🍴 The Old Creamery Sheep's Head

The Old Creamery is operated by the O'Donovan family daughters – Eleanor and Maryann. The O'Donovans have hitherto been famed for their wonderful potatoes, which, because of the unique climate of Kilcrohane, arrive to market very early in the season. The food here is simple and enticing, and do note they also supply electric bicycles for hire. *Kilcrohane, County Cork + 353 27 67139 www.theoldcreamery-sheepshead.com*

🍴 Heron Gallery & Café

Annabel Langrish has a funky café alongside her beautiful gallery, where she sells her paintings, ceramics and crafts, along with the work of other artists. If you can leave without buying an artwork you are indeed made of stern stuff. *Ahakista, County Cork + 353 27 67278 www.annabellangrish.ie. Open day time.*

🍴 Arundel's by the Pier

Arundel's bar and restaurant has a drop-dead gorgeous location, and to enjoy something delicious sitting outside at the water's edge on a sunny West Cork

Music Pub

The Tin Pub is a legendary bar just on the edge of Ahakista village, with amiable locals and lots of good music. Ahakista, County Cork + 353 27 67203

day is an experience that is hard to beat. They serve bar food downstairs, whilst the restaurant is upstairs above the bar. There are good local mussels, there are Durrus farmhouse cheese fritters and that celebrated local food hero might turn up served with smoked haddock and baby potatoes. There is Dingle crab meat in a gratin, and cod with a herb crust, and the service and value are excellent. *Ahakista, County Cork + 353 27 67033. Open lunch and dinner.*

Above: Durrus Village

Gallan Mor

Lorna and Noel's B&B is a modern, purpose-built house, but the Burkes have smartly created a new house from the old West Cork architectural vernacular, so it reads new, but feels nice and old. The house is colourful, the rooms are swaddling in their comfort and their crafty utility, and the views out across Dunmanus Bay are eye-wipingly wonderful. There is also an excellent self-catering cottage. *Kealties, Durrus, County Cork + 353 27 62732 www.gallanmor.com*

Good Things Café

Carmel Somers is one of the most imaginative and creative cooks in all of Ireland, and Good Things is an iconic destination, as you will understand when you see all the famous people who come here to eat Ms Somer's unique food. The Durrus cheese and spinach pizza is unlike anything you have ever eaten, and everything else on the menu is just as unpredictable, save for being predictably delicious. Ms Somers also runs very highly regarded cookery classes. *Durrus, County Cork + 353 27 51426 www.thegoodthingscafe.com. Open lunch and dinner seasonally.*

Blair's Cove

The setting of Blair's Cove, jutting out into Dunmanus Bay, will take your breath away when you arrive here. The cathedral-like dining room is also utterly gorgeous, and there are some fine rooms in and around the courtyard where you can stay. *Durrus, County Cork + 353 27 61127 www.blairscove.ie. Open dinner.*

Above: Good Things
Opposite: Arundel's Pub

13
Goleen,
Mizen Head and
Roaring Water Bay

Mizen Head is where things end, so they say. If you travel from one end of Ireland to the other, then you will have gone 'from Malin Head to Mizen Head' to quote the phrase. We suspect that for many travellers on the WAW, Mizen will be one of the key end-of-the-country places to make sure you get to, to make sure you tick off on the itinerary, so you can say that you climbed the 99 steps and crossed the bridge.

WILD ATLANTIC WAY

But the real reason to come to Mizen Head is not just to say you've been, instead it is to experience the exhilarating atmosphere in a place where the air seems super-charged, powered by sea salt and mighty winds, by the glint of the sunshine on the sea, by the sense of separateness, the place apart.

You feel very small indeed when in this environment, you feel very fragile next to the power of the sea and the elements in their most elemental glory. And yet, when you reflect on the lives that were lived by the signal men who used to man the lighthouse, then you also appreciate the power of the human spirit, the power to withstand isolation, the power to confront the elements, the human will to shine a light into the darkness.

Local Speciality

Gubbeen Farm-house products

The Ferguson family of Schull are amongst the best-known and most respected of Ireland's food artisans. Look out for their always busy stall at the markets in Bantry, Skibbereen and Schull over the weekends, and feast on those wonderful cheeses, salamis and peerless pork products. Their newest innovation is a very expert Irish lardo, slowly cured pork fat, which is pure gorgeous. Fingal Ferguson also makes some very, very covetable knives.

www.gubbeen.com

🍴 Along The Way

Colm and Sarah Jane Moynihan offer gorgeous scones, muffins, brownies and other lovely bakes in the morning to go with your cup of Maher's coffee, and their sandwich menu for lunchtime is really excellent and imaginative. *Old Post Office, Goleen, County Cork*

🚗 Fortview House

Here's what people say about Violet Connell's famous B&B: 'Probably the best B&B we have ever stayed in. Violet Connell is one of the nicest people you will ever meet and we loved every minute staying in this smashing house.' No more need be said about wonderful Fortview. *Gurtyowen, Toormore, Goleen, County Cork + 353 28 35324 www.fortviewhousegoleen.com.*

🍴 The Crookhaven Inn

Emma and Freddy serve smashing food in the Crookhaven Inn, and they do it calmly and don't make a fuss about it. The signature dishes are resoundingly successful – braised lamb shank with rosemary mash; fish soup with aioli; rigatoni with roasted red pepper pesto and smoked chicken; monkfish wrapped in Gubbeen pancetta. After a day at Barleycove beach, it's bliss. *Crookhaven, County Cork + 353 28 35309 www.crookhaveninn.com. Open lunch and dinner.*

🍴 O'Sullivan's Bar

The O'Sullivan family's bar is as much a part of West Cork as pastel-painted villages and the Fastnet Rock. You come here to this unique bar to chill, to have excellent sandwiches and chowder, and to see who else has come here to chill and have excellent sandwiches and chowder. *Crookhaven, County Cork + 353 28 35319 www.osullivanscrookhaven.ie. Open lunch and early evening.*

Mizen Head Visitor's Centre

You can get a cup of tea, a toasted sandwich, or bowl of seafood chowder in the Mizen Head Centre, when visiting the Mizen Head Signal Station. *Mizen Head, County Cork + 353 28 35115 www.mizenhead.net Open day time.*

Grove House

Katarina and Nico run Schull's best place to stay, and they also run Schull's best place to eat, thanks to Nico's fun, smart cooking. The ingredients are well sourced and Nico handles them with skill and flair. Value for money is really exceptional, and Katarina's warm welcome means everyone is very chilled from the moment they walk in the door. *Colla Road, Schull, County Cork + 353 28 28067 www.grovehouseschull. com. Open lunch and dinner. Booking essential.*

Hackett's

The grooviest bar in Schull has great drinks and brilliant craic along with some really punky, funky cooking – you won't get a better bowl of soup in West Cork than the Hackett's signature soups. *Main Street, Schull, County Cork + 353 28 28625. Open lunch and Fri & Saturday nights if pre booked.*

Above: Hackett's

Casa Diego

Diego and his friends make nice Spanish-accented food here at the top of Main Street. The lean rooms suit the simple elegance of the food, and it's a splendid place to feed children on good patatas bravas, paella, calamari, albondigas and their very good homemade croquettes. *Main Street, Schull, County Cork + 353 86 3978364 www.casadiego.ie. Open lunch and dinner.*

Schull Sunday Market

Schull Market is one of the best of the West Cork markets, always jammers with great food offerings from some of Ireland's most creative artisans, and it's easy to put together a special Sunday picnic lunch from the stalls.

❚❙ Antonio's

Antonio's is one of the busiest restaurants in West Cork, and its charismatic mix of good Italian food and good pizzas is a winning formula. Their signature pasta dishes are really fine, and an evening here is great theatre and great fun. *Main Street, Ballydehob, County Cork + 353 28 37139 Open lunch and dinner.*

❚❙ Hudson's

The artisan producers of West Cork beat a path to Hudson's with their produce, closely followed by Gillian Hudson's devoted customers who want to get their hands on all that lovely produce. The combination of a fine bakery, a wholefood store, a vegetable shop and a fine café makes for a one-stop-oasis of good things. *Main Street, Ballydehob, County Cork + 353 28 37565 www.hudsonswholefood.com. Open day time.*

Above: Antonio's
Below: Thornton's Organics
Opposite: Field's Supermarket

❚❙ West Cork Gourmet Store

Joanne has created a clever and enduring concept in this tiny space. Food is prepared behind a large display of charcuterie and salads; chairs are dotted around underneath shelves of oriental and Irish produce, and there is a tiny garden out back. WCGS is a place for lunch, and the occasional summer dinner. *Staball Hill, Ballydehob, County Cork + 353 28 25991 Open daily.*

❚❙ Apple Betty's

Apple Betty's is a simple and heartfelt family, community café. Fancy a coffee and a salad sandwich? Homemade shortbread biscuits, lemon drizzle? Then this is the spot for you. *The Square, Skibbereen, County Cork + 353 28 51833*

Bridge House

Mona Best runs the most idiosyncratic B&B in West Cork. If Tim Burton were to open a guesthouse, he would design it to look just like Bridge House, and Ms Best is one of the great hostesses. *Bridge Street, Skibbereen, County Cork + 353 28 21273 www.bridge-houseskibbereen.com.*

Fields of Skibbereen

John Field's supermarket is one of the greatest food stores in Europe, and every good thing that is produced in West Cork can be found here, sold with knowledge and pride by a wonderful team of people. *Main Street, Skibbereen, County Cork + 353 28 21400 www.fieldsofskibbereen.ie Open daily.*

Kalbo's

Siobhan O'Callaghan is one of the best cooks in West Cork, and everything cooked in Kalbo's has her signature of superb sourcing, and sophisticated cooking. And the chocolate brownies are the best. *48 North Street, Skibbereen, County Cork + 353 28 21515. Open daily and dinner Fri-Sat.*

West Cork Hotel

Chef Christian Pozimski and his team conjure up tasty cooking in the venerable WCH. Excellent staff make for a very fine place to stay and eat when on the WAW. *Ilen Street, Skibbereen, County Cork + 353 28 21277 www.westcorkhotel.com*

West Cork Islands

Island Cottage John Desmond and Ellmary Fenton's restaurant offers a single sitting, no-choice menu, and has been delighting food lovers for decades with an inspired formula. *Heir Island +353 28 38102 www.islandcottage.com* **Séan Rua's Restaurant and Shop** This lovely shop and restaurant has all you need if you are staying on or visiting Cape Clear. It's right at the pier, and the restaurant has a short menu — seafood chowder; mackerel fillets; mussels with leeks; seafood platter. *North Harbour, Cape Clear +353 28 39099 www.seanruas. com* **The Islander's Rest & Murphy's Pub** Sherkin is a gorgeous island, so make the most of it by taking the ferry from Baltimore and take one of the rooms in The Islander's Rest. There are frequent gigs in Murphy's Pub. *Sherkin Island +353 28 20116 www.sherkin.ie*

14
Baltimore, Toe Head & Galley Head

'Suddenly an entire galaxy of stars explodes from my fingertips, sending fading constellations of pale blue lights swirling out into the black'.

That's the travel writer Kevin Rushby, writing in *The Guardian*, about one of the most magical things that you can do when in and around this part of the WAW: take a night-time kayak trip, in order to have a galaxy of stars explode from your fingertips.

WILD ATLANTIC WAY

Or, to put it a little more scientifically, take the trip and discover the mesmerising magic that is bioluminescence: see what happens when microscopic phytoplankton release their stored-up light energy when they come into contact with your kayak paddle, or with your hand.

And that's not all you might see on a night trip. Whilst the bioluminescence accounts for the starlight in the sea, the stars overhead are magically clear and crystal-like, something that is often an incredible discovery for city dwellers, who never experience clear skies on account of street lighting. Stars above, and stars below, star-filled and bible black, and the whole experience is utterly mesmerising. 'The magical nocturnal world' is how Mr Rushby describes it.

🍴 Casey's Bar

The West Cork Brewing Co., a brand-new nano-brewery in the cellar of Casey's Pub in the hotel, is the brainchild of three friends, Kevin, Dominic and and Henry. Brewer Kevin makes 2 beers, Sherkin Lass, a pale ale, and Roaring Ruby, a red ale, and the trio debuted them late in 2014, with plans to develop the business over time. Ah, the way a Sherkin lass might look at you! *Church Strand, Baltimore, County Cork*

🛏 Inis Beg

The Boathouse at Inish Beg is one of the best known, and one of the most beautiful, places to stay anywhere in Ireland, a modernist masterpiece. But even if you can't manage to bag the Boathouse, all the houses on this lovely estate are cherishable. *Inis Beg, Baltimore, County Cork + 353 28 21745 www.inishbeg.com*

🍴 Glebe Gardens

Glebe is a little bit of heaven in West Cork, calming the soul and lifting the spirit. Tessa Perry is a great chef, and she is blessed to have some of the finest produce grown in Ireland right on the doorstep of the Glebe Gardens Café. The ingredients travel metres to her kitchen, and then Ms Perry sets about the quite profound transformations that distinguishes the very best cooks — homemade ravioli with ricotta, squash, oregano, nutmeg and a sage butter; beetroot and prosecco risotto with winter leaves; coq au vin with

Above (top and middle):
Glebe Gardens

parsnip mash; the Baltimore burger; hazelnut meringue with poached pear. To eat the food of the house and garden in the café in the garden in the wilds of West Cork is one of the most singular experiences in Irish culture. And don't miss their lovely shop, a treat in itself. *Baltimore, County Cork + 353 28 20232 www. glebegardens.com. Open day time.*

Rolf's
Johannes and Frederike have an excellent restaurant and excellent rooms in this lively and unpretentious hostelry. It's characterful and fun, and the good cooking brings in the West Cork locals as well as visitors to Baltimore.
Baltimore, County Cork + 353 28 20289 www. rolfscountryhouse.eu

Slipway
Wilmie Owen runs a pretty and winning B&B just across the road from the sea at beautiful Baltimore. *The Cove, Baltimore, County Cork + 353 28 20134 www.theslipway.com*

Mary's Ann's Bar
A justly celebrated and very commodious bar and restaurant in lovely little Castletownshend, the village with a tree in the middle of the road, and Harry Clarke windows in the church. *Castletownshend, County Cork + 353 28 36146*

The Celtic Ross Hotel
The Wycherley family's hotel is right by the side of the N71, and just outside Rosscarbery village itself. It's a professional and pristine operation, and it's an excellent base for touring the region. *Rosscarbery, County Cork + 353 23 8848722 www.celticrosshotel.com.*

Above: Kayak seaweed safaris and night paddling (see page 163) with www. atlanticseakayaking.com

Galley Head

If you have never stayed in a lighthouse before, then try to book the keeper's cottages at **Galley Head**, and you will have an unforgettable experience. Everything that happens in the Lightkeeper's cottages takes place under that beam of light, which sweeps rhythmically and powerfully, creating an unforgettable atmosphere that seems to bring an extra consciousness to everyday experiences. www.irishlandmark.com

O'Callaghan-Walsh

Martina and Sean cook and serve the best West Cork fish, and their scampi – and their mashed potato – are the stuff of legend. Sean is also one of the wittiest hosts in history, so you get a great sense of humour along with inspired fish cookery. *The Square, Rosscarbery, County Cork + 353 23 8848125. Open dinner*

Lis-Ardagh Lodge

Lis-Ardagh Lodge is an archetypal West Cork holiday destination. Set close to the romantic fishing village of Union Hall, the house serves as a base for those wishing to kayak, sail, water ski, wind surf, or fish and, thereby, get the best out of West Cork. It's the place to be for those who wish to walk the glorious West Cork coastline or discover West Cork's famous foods. Carol and Jim are the ideal hosts, looking after you better than you could have hoped. *Union Hall, County Cork + 353 28 34951 www.lis-ardaghlodge.com.*

Deasy's Harbour Bar

Caitlin Ruth is one of the best contemporary cooks in Ireland. She mixes grace and gutsiness in her cooking, so the food in Deasy's is wonderfully satisfying. But it's the global reach of her skills that leaves most other cooks in the shade: in winter she will cook pheasant, but make it into a pierogi; she continues her quest to make ling sexy

by matching it with popped amaranth; she serves chocolate pappardelle with pheasant and pheasant ragu, with a shake of gremolata to lift the flavours with a citrus note; her fish cakes are Korean, her fish soup is Thai; she pan-fries smoked mozzarella, and serves cardoon with brill. Ms Ruth's food is so funky it makes you want to dance on the tables, but be careful: don't dare to spill a drop of anything! Wizard food, wizard place. *Ring Village, Clonakilty, County Cork + 353 23 8835741. Open dinner and weekend lunch.*

Above: Deasy's

Aris

Our correspondent, Eugene, had only one word to say about the spiced beef blaa they serve in Aris: 'Brilliant!' Well, that will do nicely, and it's a typical reaction to the smartly-crafted foods and drinks served in this stylish room. *Asna Square, Clonakilty, County Cork + 353 23 8821673 www.ariscafe.com*

Dunowen House

Famous locally for a previous resident - Noel Redding, of the Jimi Hendrix Experience - Dunowen House is now a secluded luxury B&B with a restaurant that runs food events with invited local guest chefs. See their website for details of upcoming dinners.*Sands Cove, Ardfield, Clonakilty, County Cork + 353 23 8869099 www.dunowenhouse.ie*

Hart's

Aileen Hart runs one of the glories of Clon, a beautiful tea rooms with hip, adroit food that shines with care, sympathy and astuteness. Delightful, and a key element of this sweet town. *Ashe Street, Clonakilty, County Cork + 353 23 8835583. Open daily.*

Inchydoney Island Lodge & Spa

Owner Des O'Dowd and his team are rewriting the book of expectations at this fine beachside hotel, and they have one of the best crews working together that we have seen. The hotel seems to us to have matured beautifully, so that every element works compatibly, and it all adds up to a special getaway in a special setting. Mr O'Dowd and his team are careful to avoid the clichés that let down so many hotels in Ireland, so everything here is precise and professional. The refurbishment of the dining room has been a great success, and it's a sign of how this team examine every aspect and aim to improve upon it. Their special West Cork menus are a true treat, so, get away to Inchydoney. Just make sure to book enough time to let that sea air and spray get deep into your soul. *Clonakilty, County Cork + 353 23 8833143 www.inchydoneyisland.com*

Lettercollum Kitchen Project

Karen Austin published her first book late in 2014, and *The Lettercollum Cookbook* is an essential testament to the work of one of the great culinary teams in West Cork history: Karen and her partner, Con McLoughlin. For more than twenty five years, Lettercollum has been one of the defining West Cork destinations, a place where you discover transcendent food, served by people who wear

their alternative philosophy lightly. Nobody – but nobody – makes better pastry than these guys, but then everything they send out to the small collation of chairs in the café is blessed with goodness. Bridget Healy runs the counter and the room superbly, and wittily, and every bite will sate your appetite, and restore your soul. Great foods on the shelves complete a happy picture. *22 Connolly Street, Clonakilty, County Cork + 353 23 8836938 www.lettercollum.ie. Open day time.*

Richy's Bar & Bistro

Richy's is a fine local bar and bistro which has served Clonakilty faithfully for a dozen years now, and it's a very child-friendly place. *4 Wolfe Tone Street, Clonakilty, County Cork + 353 23 8821852 www.richysbarandbistro.com. Open lunch and dinner.*

Scally's SuperValu

Eugene Scally's SuperValu is one of the supreme Irish supermarkets, distinguished by the range of superb West Cork foods, and by really great service. If your only previous supermarket experiences are of ordinary stores, then walking in here is like walking into paradise, and every part is as impressive as every other aspect of Scally's. *Six Bridge, Clonakilty, County Cork + 353 23 8833088 www.supervaluclon.ie*

15
The Old Head
of Kinsale

The Old Head of Kinsale is marked on a map of the world produced by the Egyptian, Ptolemy, in the middle of the first century A.D., according to Allanah Hopkins' book *Eating Scenery: West Cork, The People & The Place*.

It is believed the information about the Old Head, and Cork city, the River Lee and Mizen Head which are also shown on the map, was given by sailors returning to the Mediterranean who had sailed the south west coast of Ireland. The Wild Atlantic Way has, then, been attracting visitors for millennia.

Elsewhere in her fine book, Ms Gallagher writes: 'When I first discovered the coast of West Cork, I thought I had found paradise, like many others before me. It seemed to be a place of infinite delights, where time had stood still, waiting for me to come along and explore.'

Many visitors experience this feeling, one of discovery, belonging and enchantment. It is intoxicating, and can be life-changing: you may simply decide that this is the paradise where you want to live, and your old life elsewhere is shaken off, and you step into the place of infinite delights.

WILD
ATLANTIC
WAY

Opposite: Fishy Fishy

Dillon's

As we go to press Richard Milnes, one of West Cork's best known chefs, is just about to open the doors of Dillon's. Expect precise and intelligent modern Irish cooking, on short menus featuring fish from day boats, home-grown vegetables and West Cork classic ingredients. *Mill Street, Timoleague + 353 23 8869609*

Monk's Lane

Gavin and Michelle had a runaway success story in 2014, and the public responded with just one word to their hip offering of food and wine in Monk's Lane: 'Gimme!' They are a spirited, unclichéd pair, and the buzz they get from their work translates into a fun-filled destination with delicious, West Cork cooking – lamb quesadillas with salsa fresca; O'Neill's sausages with mash and craft beer gravy; their signature West Cork plate; carrot, courgette, pecorino and chickpea veggie burger. Their selection of Irish and global craft beers is terrific, with the Cork brews heading up the list, and the excellent wines are available in many sizes. Monk's Lane is a simply darling destination, one of the new arrivals that further defines West Cork. *15 Mill Street, Timoleague www.monkslane.ie*

The Food Depot

Watching Diana Dodog cooking, at the food cart that she and her husband, Mike, call Food Depot, is just like watching a really fine musician play. This fluency, this elegance, translates directly into her cooking, which is assured, delicious and precise, cooking that elicits 'Wow!' responses from the first taste of the dish, whether it's a squash and chickpea curry, a Toulouse sausage wrap; pulled pork in brioche; salmon couscous. Running a top-class food cart at the end of a seaside cul-de-sac seems like a very West Cork thing to do, and Diana and Mike have the chutzpah to pull it off. This is elemental eating, where what counts is the goodness of the food, the largesse of its flavours, the honest style of this talented pair. *Courtmacsherry, County Cork + 353 85 737 4437*

Above and Opposite: The Food Depot

🛏 The Glen

If you get the chance to stay at The Glen, you will know that dealing in enchantment is what Guy and Diana do in this beautiful country house. You will know that they seem to hand out unforgettable moments and memories along with the breakfasts, along with their amazing afternoon teas. And years later, those memories will come flooding back, unbidden – the beauty of the house, the beauty of the gardens, the comfort, the welcome – and you, too, will be like the enchanted child, the cat who got the cream. The Glen gives the gift that keeps on giving. *Kilbrittain, County Cork + 353 23 8849862 www.glencountryhouse.com*

🍴 Diva Boutique Bakery Café & Deli

Shannen Keane runs Diva bakery, Diva café and Diva deli, and they are all excellent. Originally from Seattle, Ms Keane brings an American energy and relish to her work, and everything fizzes with flavour. One lunch we enjoyed here was that rare event: an utterly perfect meal that could not be faulted in any way, from the spicy lentil soup to the Mexican tortilla. The breads from the bakery are superlative, and the shop is jammed with deicious things, so you can put together a smashing picnic and head for the beach. *Main Street, Ballinspittle, County Cork + 353 21 4778465 www.divaboutiquebakery.com. Open day time.*

Glebe Country House

Glebe is a world-unto-itself. There are the gardens, and the gardens furnish the house with lots of things for breakfast and dinner; there are apartments for the entire family to stay; there are the rooms in the house. They cater for weddings, specialise in house parties, and cook delightful food for breakfast and dinner. *Ballinadee, Bandon, County Cork + 353 21 4778294 www.glebecountryhouse.ie*

Gort na Nain

Virtually everything Lucy cooks with in this vegetarian B&B comes straight from Ultan's acclaimed organic farm. It's their own honey, their own eggs, their own chutneys, breads, pastas, the whole nine yards. So, get your feet under the table with your fellow guests to enjoy baby aubergines stuffed with courgettes and toasted pine nuts; Puy lentil and garlic potatoes wrapped up in chard parcels; home-made rhubarb ripple ice cream. And then upstairs to a cosy bed. *Ballyherkin, Nohoval, County Cork + 353 21 4770647 www.gortnanain.com*

The Black Pig

Siobhan and Gavin's The Black Pig has become part of the fabric of culinary Kinsale faster than you can say gewürztraminer. Part of their success is the wonderful room – Jack Power in *The Examiner* called it 'seamless... it oozes integrity' – which is just right. And then Gavin and Siobhan bring exactly the right mix of fabulous wines, smartly curated and plated foods, and a bohemian bonhomie that makes the BP pretty darn irresistible. So, bring on the carpaccio of Ballinspittle beef; the crab and Toonsbridge ricotta ravioli; the Ballyhoura mushrooms on toast with Parmesan; the jamon bellota. The sourcing is first class, the wines are beyond good, service is adroit and informed and, as Lily Higgins has pointed out, behind every element of the Black Pig 'is a real commitment to excellence.' Excellence is where they're at. *Kinsale, County Cork + 353 21 477 4101. Open dinner.*

Opposite: Diva Boutique Bakery

Craft Brewery

Kinsale Porter

Sam and Maudeline Black brew a small range of beers in Kinsale, and you can see them at work when they conduct their brewery tours. They make a very fine Black IPA and a Kinsale Ale, and the newest arrival is The Session. There are also other beauties such as the draught-only Beoir #1, which comes in at a whopping 9% ABV.

 Blindgate House

We have always loved the design style of Maeve Coakley's Blindgate House, and the fact that its somewhat conventional exterior hides one of the most lushly designed and executed interiors of any house in this entire book. But style doesn't win out over comfort in Blindgate, and so this is a very cosy house to hang out in, and not one of those design traps that involves you suffering for someone else's art. As such, Blindgate is a terrific base for staying, relaxing and exploring, enjoying all the best of Kinsale whilst just being far enough up the hill to ensure peace and quiet when the town is at full tilt, but also allowing you to head out both eastwards and westwards through County Cork to sample the incredible varieties of the county, or maybe to begin your journey northwards on the Wild Atlantic Way. Maeve's breakfasts are just as stylish and fine as the design of the house, beautifully cooked and served, setting you up for the perfect day. *Blindgate, Kinsale, County Cork + 353 21 4777858 www.blindgatehouse.com*

Bastion

Paul McDonald and Heather Noonan have brought serious pedigrees to Bastion, and the cooking is dramatic and modern: 53 degree organic salmon with parsley brioche crumb; fillet steak with jam doughnuts; chorizo and Parmesan stuffed chicken; chocolate tart with broken pastry and Banyuls syrup. There is prosecco on tap, and a lot of hungry potential here. *Market Street, Kinsale, County Cork + 353 21 4709696*

Brunos

Bruno's is the real deal. The room is superbly atmospheric — imagine an enoteca in the Roman catacombs, with an ancient well in the centre — the bric-a-brac is marvellously funky, the wines are judiciously chosen, and the pizzas are made with a fermented sourdough starter, so they have winning flavour even before they are topped with San Marzano tomatoes and Toonsbridge mozzarella, or Jack McCarthy's black pudding with leeks, apple and pine nuts. Whilst their own Neapolitan pizza oven is a real draw, there are plenty of other smart choices – wild garlic risotto with hazelnuts; crab crostini; excellent steaks; fresh pasta with basil pesto. Sourcing is done with exacting care, and don't miss their own Italian wines, which offer excellent value. *36 Main Street, Kinsale, County Cork + 353 21 4777138*

Fishy Fishy

Writing in *The New Zealand Herald*, Peter Calder described Martin and Marie Shanahan's Fishy Fishy Café as "the most impressive seafood place I tried", and praised Mr Shanahan's "sublimely simple dishes", in particular the Fishy Fishy riff on surf and turf where scallops are topped with prosciutto and are accompanied by slices of black pudding. That is exactly the sort of finger-lickin' food that has made FF the destination address in Kinsale, and built Mr Shanahan's reputation as the best fish cook in the country. For first time visitors to Fishy Fishy, the cooking often comes as a revelation – fish can taste this delicious!? Mr Shanahan's secret lies not merely with technique, but also with his inspired sourcing, whereby the fish comes straight in off the boats, straight into the kitchen, and straight onto the plate: you simply can't eat fresher fish. *Crowley Quay, Kinsale, County Cork + 353 21 4700415 www.fishyfishy.ie*

Above: Fishy Fishy Cafe

Janey Mac

They make a strawberry scone in Janey Mac's that would raise the dead, such is its stunning sumptuousness. You bite into it, and you melt into a puddle of delight, and ask yourself how something so simple can be so utterly delicious? How do you bake a scone – a scone! – and make it such a moment of sheer joy. But it's not just the scones that will have you rushing back to JM's: the sausage rolls, for example, are things of porky beauty, and the room is colourful and charming. A real winner. *The Park, Kinsale, County Cork + 353 86 8172108 www.janeymackinsale.com*

¶¶ The Lemon Leaf Café

Tracy Keoghan has good taste. You only need to walk into the Lemon Leaf to see the work of someone who has an exacting eye, and bags of discrimination. When you learn that Ms Keoghan has a background in interior design, you can understand why the room feels so right. Even in a town with the high standards of Kinsale, the Lemon Leaf stands out as a special destination, a place that always feels welcoming, a place that makes you feel good. Of course, the excellent food and drinks, and the carefully chosen foods on the dresser, all add to the totality. That mid-morning cup of Ariosa coffee will hit the spot, but so will the carefully-concocted croque madam, or the sweet potato fishcakes with lime and coriander mayonnaise, or a classic smoked salmon, cream cheese and chive bagel. Everything is done just right, just so. *70 Main Street, Kinsale, County Cork + 353 21 4709792 www. lemonleafcafe.ie. Open day time.*

¶¶ Man Friday

Philip Horgan's Man Friday restaurant is one of the longest-established restaurants in Ireland, and is heading towards 40 years of service and 40 years of making people happy. It's classic cooking – deep-fried brie; sole on the bone; fillet steak with cream, brandy and peppercorns – and it's always welcome and fun, with great service. *Scilly, Kinsale, County Cork + 353 21 4772260 www.manfridaykinsale.ie. Open dinner.*

¶¶ Max's Wine Bar

Anne Marie and Olivier Queyva describe their restaurant as being both 'quaint' and 'professional', and that is just right, though we should also add 'unpretentious' to the roll-call of flattering adjectives. Everything marries well in this delightful set of rooms – the food; the decor with its artful bricolage; the service, which is calm, confident, and charming. The Queyvas make it look easy, and that is part of the charm of this Kinsale institution. *48 Main Street, Kinsale, County Cork + 353 21 4772443 www.maxs.ie. Open dinner.*

Quay Food Co

An excellent wholefood and specialist shop, invaluable for collecting the ingredients for a good picnic. *Market Quay, Kinsale, County Cork + 353 21 4774000 www.quayfood.com. Open day time.*

Toddie's @ The Bulman

Happily housed in the classic bar space of the Bulman, Pearse O'Sullivan's cooking in Toddie's has never been better, pulling in all his influences from a young life spent in both Trinidad and, ahem, Surrey: Trinidad-style crab gratin; Dublin Bay prawn soup with chilli, lemongrass and coriander; chicken with wasabi coleslaw. *Summercove, Kinsale, County Cork + 353 21 4777769 www.toddies.ie. Open lunch & dinner.*

INDEX

Achill Cliff House Hotel 40
Achill Island 39
Achill Sea Salt 51
Adare 118
Adrigole 145
Ahakista 154
Aillwee Cave 95
Along The Way 158
An Canteen 123
An Dún 90
An Fear Gorta 95
An Port Mor 45
Ana's Cupcakes 15
Anascaul 128
Angler's Return 59
Aniar 68
Annagry 19
Anton's 69
Antonio's 160
Apple Betty's 160
Aran Islands 90
Ard Bia at Nimmos 69
Ard na Sidhe 132
Ardara 19
Ardgroom 144
Aris 168
Aroi 115
Aroma 21
Artisan 70
Arundel's by the Pier 154
Ashe's Annascaul Black Pudding Co. 129
Ashe's Bar 123
Aughris 33
Avoca 55
Badger & Dodo 70
Ballina 34
Ballinsheen 99
Ballinspittle 174

Ballybunion 119
Ballybunion 119
Ballycastle 35
Ballyconneely 58
Ballydavid 122
Ballydehob 145
Ballylickey 148
Ballynahinch Castle 58
Ballyvaughan 95
Baltimore 164
Banba, Caffe 11
Bank House Restaurant 153
Bantry 150
Bantry Bay 147
Bantry Market 150
Barna 64
Basilico 88
Bastion 176
Bay Fish and Chips 104
Bay View 148
Beach Bar, The 33
Beach House Bar & Restaurant 13
Beach, The 53
Bean West Coffee 51
Beara Peninsula 143
Beehive Craft & Coffee Shop 40
Belharbour 94
Belmullet 36
Beltra Country Market 28
Bernie's Cupán Tae Café 153
Bervie 42
Bierhaus 69
Black Pig, The 175
Blackface Lamb 42

Blackfield 42
Blacksod 36
Blair's Cove 155
Blakes Bar 70
Blasket lamb 125
Blindgate House 176
Blue Bicycle, The 44
Blueberry Tearoom 21
Boathouse, The 135
Brasserie on the Corner 70
Bridge House 160
Bridgend 8
Brook Lane 137
Browns 6
Browns in Town 6
Bruno's 176
Builin Blasta 63
Buncrana 13
Burren Fine Food & Wine 96
Burren Gold 95
Burren Perfumery 94
Burren Smoke House 99
Burren, The 93
Café Noir 112
Caffe Banba 11
Caherdaniel 135
Cahirciveen 134
Caifé na Caolóige 122
Calvey's Restaurant 43
Canteen, The 114
Canteen, An 123
Cape Clear 161
Carndonagh 11
Carrick 20
Carrigaholt 111
Carrigart 18
Carrowholly Cheese 48

Casa Diego 159
Casey's Bar 164
Castle Murray House 20
Castlemaine 129
Castletownbere 144
Castletownshend 165
Castlewood 123
Cava Bodega 70
Celtic Ross Hotel,
  The 165
Chalet, The 43
Chart House 124
Cherry Blossom
  Bakery 51
Chi 72
Claire The Bakers 12
Claire's Tearooms 88
Clare Jam Company 100
Clare, County 89
Clarinbridge 89
Clarke's Seafood
  Delicatessen 34
Cleggan Seaweed Co 54
Clew Bay Hotel 46
Clifden 55
Cliffs of Moher 101
Clonakilty 168
Clonmany 12
Cloon Keen Atelier 82
Coach House Hotel 88
Coach Lane 28
Cocoa Bean Artisan
  Chocolates 140
Connaught Hotel 72
Connemara 53
Connemara Coast
  Hotel 64
Connemara Hamper 55
Connemara Hill
  Lamb 57

Connemara Smoke
  House 58
Considine's Bread 105
Copper Kettle 144
Cork, County 143
Cornstore 112
Counter, The 14
Courthouse, The 22
Courtmacsherry 172
Cove, The 18
Cratloe Hills 95
Cromane 133
Crookhaven 158
Crookhaven Inn 144
Cross Street, 7 72
Cucina, La 115
Cuinneog Butter 39
Culdaff 11
Cullinan's Restaurant &
  Guest House 100
Custom House, The 7
Da Roberta 66
Dail Bar 75
Dan Phil's Restaurant
  148
Danny Minnie's 19
Darcy's 120
Days Bar and B&B 53
Deasy's Harbour
  Bar 167
Dela 74
Delight 74
Delphi Lodge 54
Derry 6
Diamond Rocks 106
Dillon's 172
Dingle 123
Dingle Cookery
  School 123
Dingle Distillery 122

Dingle Peninsula 121
Dingle Reel Fish Co 124
Diva Boutique Bakery
  Café & Deli 174
Doherty's Café 9
Dolphin Beach 55
Donegal Islands 11
Donegal Rapeseed Oil 19
Donegal Town 17, 21
Donegal, County 8
Donnelly's of Barna 64
Doolin 100
Doonbeg 106
Dough Bros, The 74
Dozzina, Pizza 66
Dromagowlane House
  145
Drumcliffe 27
Drumcliffe Tea House 27
Drumcloc House 153
Drumquinna Manor
  Glamping 135
Dunfanaghy 17, 18
Dunkineely 20
Dunowen House 168
Durrus 155
Durrus Cheese 148
Dursey Deli 144
Eagle Point Camping 148
Eala Bhan Restaurant 28
Eden Crest 150
Egan's 104
1826 Adare 118
Eileen's Bar 154
Eithna's By The Sea 25
Emlagh House 124
Entrepans 69
Erris Head 25
Eyeries 144
Fabio's 29

Fahan 13
Fanad Peninsula 5
Fanore 101
Fields of Skibbereen 160
Figart 17
Filligan's Preserves 13
Fish at the Marina 125
Fish Kitchen 150
Fishy Fishy 177
Flaggy Shore, The 93
Food Depot 172
Fortview House 158
Foyle Bridge 5
Freddy's Bistro 113
Front Door 75
Furbo 64
Gallan Mor 155
Galley Head 166
Galley Head Lighthouse 166
Galway Bay 61
Galway City 68
Galway City Museum 79
Galway, County 53
Galway's Saturday Market 69
Gasta Good'n'Healthy 113
Glasshouse, The 29
Glebe Country House 174
Glebe Gardens 164
Glen House, The 12
Glen, The 174
Glencarrig B&B 111
Glengarriff 148
Glenties 13
Global Village 125
Goat Street Bistro 126
Goleen 158
Good Things Café 155
Goodness Cakes 74

Gorman's Clifftop House 122
Gort na Nain 175
Gourmet Greenway, The 42
Gourmet Parlour 29
Gourmet Tart Company 66
Goya's 75
Grange 27
Granny's Coffee House 94
Green Man, The 17
Greencastle 9
Greenmount 126
Gregan's Castle 96
Griffin's Bakery 77
Grove House 159
Gubbeen 158
Guild 6
Guildhall, Derry 6
Hackett's 159
Harbour, The 22
Hargadon's 30
Harrington's 145
Harry's Bar & Gastro Pub 28
Harry's Restaurant 9
Harry's Saturday Market 8
Hart's 169
Harvest Moon 51
Hawthorn House 137
Hazel Mountain Chocolates 94
Heatons 126
Heffernan's Fine Foods 34
Heifer & Hen Café 34
Heir Island 161

Heron Gallery & Café 154
Heron's Rest, The 77
Hotel Doolin 100
House Hotel, The 77
Hudson's 160
Huntsman, The 78
Idás 127
Idle Wall, The 46
Il Vicolo 87
Inchydoney 168
Independent Brewing 63
Inis Beg 164
Inis Meáin Restaurant and Suites 90
Inishbofin 53
Inishowen 5
Inniscrone 34
Irish Atlantic Sea Salt 144
Iskeroon 135
Island Cottage 161
Islander's Rest 161
Islands of West Cork 161
Jack & Eddie's 51
Jack's 133
Jack's Coastguard Restaurant 133
Jam 137
Janey Mac 177
John R's 119
Josie's Lakeview House Restaurant 140
Kai Café + Restaurant 79
Kalbos 160
Kappa Ya 79
Kate McCormack & Sons 47
Kate's Kitchen 30
Kate's Place 88
Kealy's Seafood Bar 9
Keel 40

Keem Bay Fish Products 43
Keem Bay Smoked Fish 51
Kelly Kettle, The 43
Kelly's Butchers 44
Kelly's Kitchen 44
Kenmare 135
Kenmare Select 139
Kennedy, Jerry 125
Kerry Head 117
Kerry, County 107
Kettle of Fish 79
Kilbaha 109
Kilbaha Gallery 109
Kilbrittain 172
Kilcolgan 89
Kilcornan 118
Kilcrohane 154
Kilcullen's Hot Water Seaweed Bath 30
Kilkee 106
Kilkee Golf Club 106
Killeen Farmhouse Cheese 65
Killimer Ferry 118
Killorglin 132
Kilmurvey House 90
Kilshanny 95
Kingdom Food & Wine 120
Kinlough 22
Kinnegar Craft Brewery 15
Kinsale 175
Kinsale Porter 176
Kinvara 89
Kinvara Market 89
Kitchen, The @ Galway City Museum 79

Knockranny House Hotel 46
Kylemore 55
Kylemore Abbey 55
L'Arco 95
Lahinch 104
Lang's of Grange 27
Lauragh 140
Leenane 54
Legenderry Warehouse Number One 6
Léim Siar 36
Lemon Leaf Café 178
Lettercollum Kitchen Project 169
Letterfrack 54
Letterfrack Lodge 54
Letterkenny 14
Lime Tree 137
Limerick 112
Limerick Milk Market 115
Linnalla Ice Cream 94
Lir 106
Lis-Ardagh Lodge 166
Liscannor 103
Liscannor Bay 99
Lisdoonvarna 99
Listowel 119
Little Cheese Shop 116
Loam 80
Lodge, The 43
Long Dock, The 111
Loop de Loop 145
Loop Head 106
Loop Head Lighthouse 111
Lorge Chocolates 140
Lough Swilly 15

Louis Mulcahy 122
Loveachill.com 40
Lyon's Café 30
Ma Murphy's 151
Malin Head 11
Mallmore Country House 56
Malt House, The 81
Man Friday 178
Manna 120
Manning's Emporium 148
Market Fifty Seven 47
Market Kitchen 35
Marlene's Chocolate Haven 47
Martine's Quay Street Wine Bar 82
Mary-Anne's Tea Rooms 120
Mary's Ann's Bar 165
Mary's Cottage Kitchen 35
Massimo 81
Matt Molloy's 47
Max's Wine Bar 178
Maxwell's Restaurant 83
Mayo, County 39
McCambridge's 81
McCarthy's Bar 145
McCormack, Kate & Sons 47
McDonagh's Seafood House 82
McGeough's Butchers 67
McGrory's 11
McMunn's of Ballybunion 119
Merchant House, The 6
Mescan 44
Mill Restaurant, The 17

Milleens Cheese 143
Milltown 129
Milltown House 128
Milltown Market 129
Miner's Red Ale 17
Mitchell's Restaurant 56
Mizen Head 157
Mizen Head Visitor's Centre 159
Monks Lane 172
Moorings, The 134
Moran's Oyster Cottage 89
Morrisseys 106
Mortell's 113
Morton's of Galway 66
Mount Callan 95
Mountcharles 21
Moy House 105
Muckish Mountain Brewery 17
Mulberry's 64
Mulcahy, Louis 122
Mulcahy's 138
Mullaghmore 25
Mullet Peninsula 25
Mulranny 40
Mulranny Park 40
Murphy Blacks 108
Murphy's Ice Cream 128
Murrevagh Honey 51
Nancy's Bar 19
Naughton's Bar 108
New Quay 94
Newport 44
Newport House 45
Nick's 132
No Thirty Five 138
Norman Villa 67
Number One Pery Sq 112

O'Callaghan-Walsh 166
O'Dowd's Seafood Bar & Restaurant 59
O'Grady's on the Pier 65
O'Lochlainn's Bar 96
O'Looneys on the Prom 105
O'Neill's The Point Bar 134
O'Sullivan's Bar 159
Oileán Ruaidh 11
Old Creamery Sheep's Head 154
Old Head of Kinsale 171
Old Schoolhouse B&B 110
Olde Castle Bar & Restaurant 22
Olde Glen Bar and Restaurant 18
On the Wild Side 120
Oranmore 88
Organico 151
Oscar's 83
Oslo 67
Osta 32
Out of the Blue 128
Packie's 138
Paddy Coyne's Bar 55
Pantry and Corkscrew 48
Pantry Shop & Bakery 109
Park Hotel 139
Parknasilla 135
Pax House 129
Peg's Shop 145
Petit Delice 83
Petites Douceurs 81
Phoenix, The 119
Pilot Bar, The 34

Piog Pies 116
Pizza Dozzina 66
Polke's 35
Port Mor, An 45
Port na Blagh 18
Portmagee 134
Providence Market Kitchen 83
Pure Magic at the Lodge 43
Purecamping 111
Purple Heather 139
Pyke 'n' Pommes 6
QCs 134
Quay Cottage 50
Quay Food Co 179
Quay House 57
Quinlan's Seafoods 121
Rathcormac 27
Rathmullan 15
Rathmullan House 15
Recess 58
Red Door, The 13
Red's Sauces 51
Renvyle 54
Renvyle House Hotel 54
Restaurant 1826 Adare 118
Rhonwen's Eateries Bistro 144
Richy's Bar & Bistro 169
Rigney's Farm 118
Ring of Beara 143
Ring of Kerry 131
Ring Village 167
Roadford House 100
Roadside Tavern 99
Roast House, The 121
Roberta, da 66
Rolf's 165

Rosleague Manor 55
Rosscarbery 165
Rosses Point 28
Roundstone 59
Royal Villa, The 67
Russell Gallery 95
Rustic Grub 89
Saddler's House, The 6
Sage Westport 51
Sailor's Bar 140
Salthill 66
Salthouse, The 85
Scally's Supervalu 169
Scarpello & Co. 8, 15
Schull 159
Schull Sunday
  Market 159
Sea Mist House 57
Sea View House
  Doolin 101
Sea View House
  Hotel 149
Seacrest Guest House 25
Séan Rua's Restaurant
  161
Seaweed Company,
  Cleggan 54
Sheedy's Hotel 99
Sheep's Head 153
Sheep's Head Producers
  154
Shelburne Lodge 139
Shell's Café and Little
  Shop 32
Sheridan's
  Cheesemongers 84
Sherkin Island 161
Skelligs Chocolate
  Company 140
Skibbereen 160

Slea Head 122
Sligo 28
Sligo Bay 25
Sligo, County 25
Slipway 150
Sneem 135
Snug, The 139
Sol Rio 48
Sol y Sombra 132
Solaris Teas 70
South Pole Inn 128
Spa Seafoods 121
Spiddal 63
St Tola 91
Starfish Café and
  Bistro 18
Stella Maris, Clare 109
Stella Maris, Mayo 35
Stop B&B 85
Strand Bar 32
Strand, The, Kilkee 109
Strandhill 32
Strandhill Lodge &
  Suites 33
Stuffed Olive 152
Sundaes Ice Cream
  Parlour 119
Talbot Hotel 36
Tap Room, The 15
Tarbert Ferry 118
Taste 145
Taste of Days Gone By 51
Tavern, The 51
Teelin 20
Thalassotherapy Centre
  Guest House 110
Thirty Seven West 84
Tí Linn 20
Tide Full Inn, The 89
Tigh Neachtain 84

Timoleague 172
Tin Pub, The 154
Toddie's @ The Bulman
  179
Toe Head 163
Tory Island 11
Tralee 109
Tulsi 85
Twelve Hotel, The 64
Union Hall 166
Upstairs @ West 65
Valentia Ice-cream 132
Vanilla Grape 140
Vasco 101
Vaughan Lodge 104
Vaughan's Anchor
  Inn 104
Vicolo, Il 87
Village Tavern, The 20
Vina Mara 87
Vintage Lane 27
Wa Café 87
West 65
West Cork Gourmet
  Store 160
West Cork Hotel 161
West End Café 19
West Kerry Brewery 121
West Mayo Brewery 47
Westport 45
Westport Plaza Hotel 50
Wharton's 140, 151
Whiddy Island 153
Wild Geese 118
Wild Honey Inn 99
Wild Irish Sea Veg 96
Wild Mint Deli 43
Wild Onion, The 115
Wildwood Vinegars 51
Zest Café 133

WILD ATLANTIC WAY
SLÍ AN ATLANTAIGH FHIÁIN

About the Wild Atlantic Way:

The Wild Atlantic Way is Ireland's first long-distance touring route, stretching from the Foyle Bridge in Derry, through the Inishowen Peninsula, and then travelling along the entire western coastline, ending 2,500km later, in Kinsale in County Cork.

The route is well-signposted throughout, and includes various loop routes and discovery points. Maps of the route are available on-line, and maps and more information about the route can be found from the Irish tourist board websites, including: www.ireland.com/wild-atlantic-way.

About McKennas' Guides:

We have been publishing food and accommodation guides to Ireland for over twenty-five years, and have won local and international awards for our publications. Look out for our silver plaques on recommended establishments.

Our publications also include a range of digital options as well as this book on Where to Eat and Stay on the Wild Atlantic Way.

Look out for and download our Apps: the 100 Best Restaurants in Ireland. We also publish the 100 Best Places to Stay in Ireland, as well as a digital Smart Guide that puts this book on an App, and brings you all the connectivity associated with that medium.

Our website www.guides.ie lists all the activities and publications connected with *McKennas' Guides*, and contains many recommendations for great places to eat and stay and wonderful local Irish foods.

We also publish a Who's Who of Irish food. Other things that are published through our website include:

Megabites is a regular on-line digital magazine that you can subscribe to from the website www.guides.ie. Let us deliver it to your inbox, and it is free.

The Irish Food Channel is our independent video channel featuring people in food from all around the country. Takeaway is our podcast, details from our website.

We are on Facebook www.facebook.com/BridgestoneGuides and www.facebook.com/wheretoeatandstayonthewildatlanticway. Check here for updates on everything to do with the WAW.

We are on Twitter with @McKennasGuides and Instagram with Sally McKenna.